The Real FORTINET® Cookbook

The Real FORTINET® Cookbook

A MODERN COOKBOOK

COMPILED BY THE
FORTINET US MARKETING TEAM

PALMETTO
PUBLISHING

Charleston, SC
www.PalmettoPublishing.com

The Real Fortinet Cookbook

First Edition

Paperback ISBN: 979-8-8229-0527-6

CONTENTS

FOREWORD vii

BREAKFAST 1

STARTERS 23

MAINS 39

SIDES 105

DRINKS 127

DESSERTS 141

FOREWORD

Let's be very clear: If you're expecting a typical technical and dry cookbook on the following pages, the team at Fortinet has a surprise for you. In fact, the driest thing that could come out of this book is if you overcook the pork chops on page 46.

The true story around this book began in 2021. To keep ourselves engaged with each other during the pandemic (and entertained, too), the Fortinet US marketing team began the project of sharing recipes. We were all stuck at home cooking anyway, so why not expand our palates with recommendations from our most trusted colleagues? The result of that effort is this book—curated with love from those who love Fortinet...and eating too!

—The Fortinet US marketing team

BREAKFAST

AVOCADO AND GOAT CHEESE OMELETTE

By Pauline Lacroix

SERVES: 2 | PREP TIME: 7 MINUTES | COOK TIME: 5 MINUTES

INGREDIENTS

6 eggs
Salt and pepper, to taste
Cooking spray or 1 tablespoon olive oil
2 heaping tablespoons goat cheese
½ ripe avocado, sliced
15 multicolored cherry tomatoes, sliced in halves

INSTRUCTIONS

1. Whisk eggs together, and season with salt and pepper.
2. Spray a small skillet with cooking spray (or use a tablespoon of olive oil), and heat over medium heat
3. Add the egg mixture, and cook it till the mixture is cooked (about 3 minutes).
4. Add the goat cheese and avocado, fold the omelette, and then turn off the heat. Wait 2 minutes for the cheese to heat up.
5. Remove the omelette from the stove. Cut it into 2 pieces, and serve it with the halved cherry tomatoes on top.

AVOCADO CRISTO WITH CHERRY TOMATO JAM AND BALSAMIC REDUCTION

Chef Brent Wertz, Mohonk Mountain House; Adapted by Bonnie Sparkman

SERVES: 4–6 | PREP TIME: 40 MINUTES | COOK TIME: 15 MINUTES

INGREDIENTS

6–8 eggs, lightly beaten
3 ounces milk
2 garlic cloves, minced
1 teaspoon cumin
Salt and pepper
1 loaf sourdough bread, cut in ½" slices
Olive oil (for greasing)
2 avocados, peeled and sliced
6 ounces Monterey Jack

Tips

- Don't have sourdough? Challah or brioche bread works great too!
- If you prefer heavily battered bread, increase the number of eggs and milk. I prefer to just lightly dip the bread.

The Cherry Tomato Jam

1 pound cherry tomatoes, chopped
2 ounces sugar (You may want to use less depending on the sweetness of your tomatoes!)

Balsamic Reduction

6 ounces aged balsamic vinegar

Tip: Pressed for time? Use balsamic glaze from Trader Joe's or Roland Foods.

Final Touches

1 tablespoon lime juice (optional)

1 bunch cilantro, chopped

2 avocados, peeled and sliced

INSTRUCTIONS

1. Preheat the oven to 375°F.
2. In a medium size bowl, combine the eggs, milk, garlic, cumin, and salt and pepper, and lightly beat the mixture. Dip the bread slices in the egg mixture, covering both sides.
3. In a baking dish lightly coated with olive oil, place a layer of bread slices on the bottom. Arrange a layer of avocado slices in a fan design on top of the bread. Cover with a layer of Monterey Jack. Place another layer of the dipped bread slices over the cheese and avocados.
4. Bake it in the oven for 15 minutes, or until the bread is nicely browned.

Tips

- You can either arrange the bread randomly, like a casserole, or you can align it for more of a sandwich feel, as shown in the picture.

(cont'd)

- If it’s not browning, turn on the broiler for less than 1 minute. (Keep an eye on it!)

5. To make the cherry tomato jam, sauté the cherry tomatoes and sugar in a pan until the liquid reduces and thickens. Set it aside to cool.
6. In a medium-size pot, reduce the balsamic vinegar until it has slightly thickened. Set it aside to cool slightly.
7. To serve, remove the Avocado Cristo from the baking dish, and cut it into wedges. Arrange the wedges on serving plates with the cherry tomato jam and a drizzle of the balsamic reduction. Garnish the plates with lime juice (if using), chopped cilantro, and 1–3 slices of avocado.

BANANA-APPLE-CARROT POWER MUFFINS

By Karen Warnick

SERVES: 14 | PREP TIME: 20–30 MINUTES | COOK TIME: 25 MINUTES

INGREDIENTS

2 cups oat flour
½ cup almond flour
½ cup whole rolled oats
¼ cup chia seeds
2 teaspoons baking powder
½ teaspoon baking soda
1 teaspoon cinnamon
½ teaspoon nutmeg
½ teaspoon salt
3 medium, ripe bananas
⅓ cup nut butter (I prefer almond, but you can sub any nut/soy butter)
⅓ cup honey
½ cup nondairy unsweetened milk (I prefer soy)
1 teaspoon pure vanilla extract
1 medium carrot, shredded (I use a cheese grater)
1 large, green Granny Smith apple, shredded (I use a cheese grater)
⅓ cup chopped walnuts (optional)

INSTRUCTIONS

1. Preheat the oven to 350°F, and line/grease a muffin tin.
2. In a large bowl, combine and stir the oat flour, almond flour, oats, chia seeds, baking powder, baking soda, cinnamon, nutmeg, and salt.
3. In another large bowl, mash the bananas until they do not have any large banana chunks. Add the nut butter and honey, and mix together. Then add the nondairy milk and vanilla. Mix the mixture together until the wet ingredients are thoroughly combined.
4. Slowly add the combined dry ingredients in small increments to the wet batter, mixing until all is well incorporated.
5. Fold in the carrots, apples, and walnuts (if using).
6. Scoop about ⅓ cup of batter into each muffin mold. (I use an ice cream scooper.) Bake at 350°F for 24–26 minutes. The muffins will be firm to the touch and slightly golden.

(cont'd)

7. Remove the muffins from the oven, and let them sit in the muffin tin for 10–15 minutes. Then transfer the muffins to a cooling rack.

Tips

- Store the muffins in the refrigerator, tightly covered, for up to four days. (They are typically gone before four days in my house!) Or store them in the freezer for up to three months. I typically double the recipe and freeze a batch to have on hand.
- These muffins are perfect for breakfast or a power snack or to refuel yourself after a workout. They are full of nutrients, omega-3 fat, antioxidants, potassium, and fiber—plus they have 7.5 grams of protein in each muffin! They are also gluten-free, dairy-free, and egg-free.

BANANA-BLUEBERRY POWER MUFFINS

By Karen Warnick

SERVES: 14 | PREP TIME: 20–30 MINUTES | COOK TIME: 25 MINUTES

INGREDIENTS

2 cups oat flour
½ cup almond flour
½ cup whole rolled oats
¼ cup chia seeds
2 teaspoons baking powder
½ teaspoon baking soda
1 teaspoon cinnamon
½ teaspoon nutmeg
½ teaspoon salt
3 medium, ripe bananas
⅓ cup nut butter (I prefer almond, but you can sub any nut/soy butter)
⅓ cup honey
½ cup nondairy unsweetened milk (I prefer soy)
1 teaspoon pure vanilla extract
1 cup blueberries, fresh or frozen (You can sub any berries, but blueberries are my family's favorite)
⅓ cup chopped walnuts (optional)

INSTRUCTIONS

1. Preheat the oven to 350°F, and line/grease a muffin tin.
2. In a large bowl, combine and stir the oat flour, almond flour, oats, chia seeds, baking powder, baking soda, cinnamon, nutmeg, and salt.
3. In another large bowl, mash the bananas until they do not have any large banana chunks. Add the nut butter and honey, and mix together. Then add the nondairy milk and vanilla. Mix the mixture together until the wet ingredients are thoroughly combined.
4. Slowly add the combined dry ingredients in small increments to the wet batter, mixing until all is well incorporated.
5. Fold in the blueberries and walnuts (if using).
6. Scoop about ⅓ cup of batter into each muffin mold. (I use an ice cream scooper.) Bake at 350°F for 24–26 minutes. The muffins will be firm to the touch and slightly golden.

(cont'd)

7. Remove the muffins from the oven, and let them sit in the muffin tin for 10–15 minutes. Then transfer the muffins to a cooling rack.

Tips

- Store the muffins in the refrigerator, tightly covered, for up to four days. (They are typically gone before four days in my house!) Or store them in the freezer for up to three months. I typically double the recipe and freeze a batch to have on hand.
- These muffins are perfect for breakfast or a power snack or to refuel yourself after a workout. They are full of nutrients, omega-3 fat, antioxidants, potassium, and fiber—plus they have 7.5 grams of protein in each muffin! They are also gluten-free, dairy-free, and egg-free.

BAKERY-STYLE BLUEBERRY MUFFINS

By Amanda Anderson

SERVES: 12 | PREP TIME: 10 MINUTES | COOK TIME: 20 MINUTES

INGREDIENTS

½ cup butter, softened
1 egg
1 cup sugar
2 cups flour
2 teaspoons baking powder
½ teaspoon salt, if using unsalted butter
1 cup blueberries

INSTRUCTIONS

1. Preheat the oven to 350°F.
2. Mix the softened butter, egg, and sugar with a pastry cutter or fork. (Do not use a mixer; mix by hand.)
3. Add the flour and baking powder (and salt, if needed).
4. Once mixed, fold in the blueberries. The mixture will be very crumbly and flaky—this is normal.
5. Spoon the mixture into a lined muffin pan. Bake for 20–22 minutes.

CABIN PANCAKES

By Brianna Fischer

SERVES: 2 | PREP TIME: 7 MINUTES | COOK TIME: 5 MINUTES

INGREDIENTS

1 cup flour
1 ½ tablespoons sugar
1 tablespoon baking powder
½ teaspoon baking soda
½ teaspoon salt
1 tablespoon vanilla
2 tablespoons butter, melted (plus additional butter for grilling)
1 egg
1 cup milk

INSTRUCTIONS

1. In a large bowl, mix all the dry ingredients: the flour, sugar, baking powder, baking soda, and salt.
2. Add in the vanilla, melted butter, and egg.
3. Slowly whisk in the milk. (For thicker pancakes, add less milk; for thinner pancakes, add more milk.)
4. Grab a griddle or frying pan, and heat it on medium-low heat. Once it's hot, add a little bit of butter onto the pan, and wait for it to melt.
5. Pour or scoop the batter onto the griddle or frying pan. Once you see bubbles forming, it's time to flip!
6. Enjoy!

GERMAN (DUTCH BABY) PANCAKES

By Courtney Radke

SERVES: 3–4 | PREP TIME: 10 MINUTES | COOK TIME: 12–18 MINUTES

NOTES

- You will need a cast-iron skillet. (A 9", 11", or 13" works. The cakes will just be thinner the bigger you go.)
- Preheat the skillet if preferred.
- Use all-purpose flour to ensure the cake rises.
- You can substitute or remove the vanilla extract to suit your taste!

"I usually double up the ingredients and make a large and small cake so I can play with the ingredients!"

INGREDIENTS

3 large eggs
½ cup milk
3 tablespoons unsalted butter, melted (divided)
¼ teaspoon salt
1 tablespoon sugar
½ teaspoon vanilla extract (or to taste)
½ cup all-purpose flour
Fruit and toppings of your choice!

INSTRUCTIONS

1. Preheat the oven to 450°F, and, optionally, place the skillet in to preheat.
2. Grab a medium or large bowl, and get to mixing! Mix the eggs first, being careful not to over whisk. Then add the milk, 2 tablespoons of the melted butter, salt, and sugar (and vanilla, if using) to the bowl, and continue whisking.
3. Add the flour, a little at a time, and continue to stir until incorporated. Don't overmix; a few chunks of flour is just fine.

(cont'd)

4. Coat the bottom of the skillet with the rest of the melted butter, making sure to thoroughly coat the bottom and the sides. I like to take a square of unmelted butter and line the sides.
5. Pour the batter into the skillet, and bake for 12–18 minutes or until the edges start to turn golden brown. (Don't worry if it starts to look like the surface of the moon! All part of the process.)

6. Remove it from the oven, being careful—the skillet will be *hot*! Let it rest for a moment to let the top lower and to allow the custard to set.
7. Cut it into slices, and garnish it with your favorite toppings. I recommend fresh fruit, warm maple syrup, and powdered sugar. And *enjoy!*

"My family absolutely loves this quick and easy breakfast (or dinner) recipe, and we have had fun playing with the ingredients. (Spiced rum, anyone?) We hope you enjoy it as well!"

LIGHT LEMONY CREPES

By Maria Jacobson

SERVES: 4–6 | PREP TIME: 10 MINUTES | INACTIVE: 2 HOURS | COOK TIME: 10 MINUTES

INGREDIENTS

The Crepes

1 cup flour

⅔ cup water

⅔ cup milk

3 eggs

3 tablespoons butter, melted (plus more for the pan)

1 tablespoon granulated sugar

The Toppings

1 tablespoon powdered sugar

1 lemon, sliced

Fresh berries on the side

INSTRUCTIONS

1. Combine the flour, water, milk, eggs, and melted butter in a medium mixing bowl. Whisk until smooth. Stir in the sugar.
2. Cover the batter, and place it in the fridge for at least 2 hours to give the flour time to expand.
3. Add about 1 tablespoon of butter to a medium-size frying pan, and place it over medium heat. Allow the pan to fully heat before adding the batter.
4. Place 2–3 tablespoons of batter into the hot pan, and gently swirl the pan in circular motions, creating a thin layer spread evenly on the pan. (You can practice on the first couple of crepes and snack on them while you finish cooking the rest.)

(cont'd)

5. Cook about 1–2 minutes per side. Cooking time will vary based on the skillet, stove top, and how thin the crepe is. You'll know they're done when you see a lacey, golden brown finish.
6. Using a small sieve, sprinkle the crepes with the powdered sugar, followed by a squeeze of fresh lemon juice.
7. Serve the crepes with fresh berries and your favorite coffee or tea!

PECAN FRENCH TOAST

By Tricia Richardson

SERVES: 6–8 | PREP TIME: 15 MINUTES | COOK TIME: 25 MINUTES

INGREDIENTS

The French Toast

1 loaf French bread

4 eggs

2 cups whole milk

1 teaspoon cinnamon

1 tablespoon vanilla extract

½ cup sugar

3 tablespoons butter

Crumb Topping

¼ cup brown sugar

¼ cup butter, softened

¼ cup oats

½ teaspoon cinnamon

¼ cup pecans, chopped

INSTRUCTIONS

Night Before

1. Prepare a large 10" × 15" baking dish lightly with coating spray.
2. Cut the bread into 1 ½" slices. Place the slices in the baking dish.
3. In a small bowl, whisk the eggs, milk, cinnamon, vanilla, and sugar.
4. Pour the mixture over the bread slices.
5. Flip over each slice after the egg mixture is partially absorbed.
6. When all the mixture is absorbed, top each slice with a thin pat of butter.
7. Wrap the baking dish tightly with plastic wrap, and freeze for 8–10 hours.

(cont'd)

Next Morning

1. Remove baking dish from the freezer, and remove the plastic wrap.
2. Preheat the oven to 500°F.
3. Bake the dish 15 minutes.
4. In the meantime, make the crumb topping. Combine all the topping ingredients so everything is coated.
5. Remove the pan from the oven.
6. Flip the pieces over.
7. Add the crumb topping, and return the dish to bake an additional 10 minutes.
8. Serve with real maple syrup and, yes, more butter.

"Your guests will never want to leave, so be careful who you make this for!"

SIMPLE ONE-POT BANANA BREAD

By Janette Gawlikowski

SERVES: 4–8 | PREP TIME: 15–20 MINUTES | COOK TIME: 50–60 MINUTES

INGREDIENTS

3–6 very ripe bananas, mashed (about 1 ¼–2 cups)
⅓ cup butter, unsalted or salted, melted
½ teaspoon baking soda
1 pinch salt
¾ cup sugar (or 1 cup if you like it sweet)
1 egg, beaten
1 teaspoon vanilla extract
1 ½ cups all-purpose flour

INSTRUCTIONS

1. Preheat the oven to 350°F, and butter a 4" × 8" loaf pan.
2. In a large mixing bowl, mash the bananas with a fork until smooth. Stir in the melted butter.
3. Mix the baking soda and salt into the mashed bananas. Then mix in the sugar, egg, and vanilla extract.
4. Carefully mix in the flour, stirring only just enough, to avoid chewy bread—no more than 35–45 stirs.
5. Pour the batter into the prepared loaf pan. Cook for 50–60 minutes at 350°F. The bread is ready when a skewer inserted in middle comes out clean.
6. Remove the bread from the oven, and let it cool for 5 minutes. Then remove it from the loaf pan, and let it cool for another 10–15 minutes—if you can wait that long!
7. Slice and enjoy!

(cont'd)

Tips

- If the outside browns but the middle is still wet, tent the loaf with aluminum foil and continue baking until ready.
- The loaf may be stored at room temp for up to four days or in the refrigerator for up to five days.

TATER TOT BREAKFAST CASSEROLE

By Heather Andrews

SERVES: 4–6 | PREP TIME: 10 MINUTES | COOK TIME: 45–50 MINUTES

INGREDIENTS

1 pound breakfast sausage
2 cups cheddar cheese, shredded
2 cups milk
2 eggs
Salt and pepper
1 28-ounce package frozen tater tots

INSTRUCTIONS

1. Preheat the oven to 425°F.
2. Cook the sausage. (If you can't find "breakfast sausage," I've also used regular Jimmy Dean sausage.)
3. Put the cooked sausage on the bottom of a 9" × 13" pan.
4. Layer the cheese on top of the sausage.
5. Mix the milk and eggs together, adding some salt and pepper to taste, and pour the mixture over the sausage and cheese.
6. Top the mixture with the entire bag of tater tots.
7. Bake it for 45–50 minutes, until the top is nicely browned and you see bubbling in the corners.
8. Try not to eat the entire thing yourself!

STARTERS

COCONUT-CRAB CAKES WITH LEMON MAYONNAISE

By Tricia Richardson

SERVES: 4 | PREP TIME: 15 MINUTES | COOK TIME: 15 MINUTES

INGREDIENTS

The Lemon Mayonnaise

1 cup mayonnaise

Juice from ½ a lemon

The Crab Cakes

1 pound fresh crab meat

½ cup unsweetened coconut, finely grated

⅓ cup panko bread crumbs

2 large eggs, lightly beaten

2 tablespoons cilantro, freshly chopped

1 teaspoon curry powder

1 teaspoon fresh lime juice

½ teaspoon fresh ginger, finely grated

½ teaspoon jalapeño, minced

½ teaspoon fresh garlic, minced

½ teaspoon salt

¼ teaspoon coriander, ground

¼ teaspoon cumin, ground

¼ teaspoon cayenne pepper

2 tablespoons oil for sautéing

INSTRUCTIONS

The Lemon Mayonnaise

1. Combine the mayonnaise and lemon juice in a mixing bowl, and whisk until smooth.

(cont'd)

The Crab Cakes

1. In a large bowl, combine all ingredients (except for the oil), and toss gently.
2. Shape the mixture by ½ cup handfuls into 8 cakes, each about 2 ½" in diameter.
3. Place the crab cakes on a cookie sheet, and refrigerate them for 15 minutes.
4. Heat 2 tablespoons oil in a nonstick pan or cast-iron skillet.
5. Sauté the crab cakes until golden brown, roughly 3–4 minutes on each side. Then drain them on paper towels.
6. Serve the crab cakes with the lemon mayonnaise and a side salad as a light dinner. Delish!

CREAM OF ASPARAGUS SOUP

By Laura Lee

SERVES: 4–5 | PREP TIME: 5 MINUTES | COOK TIME: 20 MINUTES

INGREDIENTS

1 bunch asparagus
2 tablespoons butter
1 small onion, chopped
1 tablespoon garlic, minced (or, if you are like me, a heaping spoonful)
Salt and pepper (to taste)
3 cups chicken broth
1 cup heavy cream
1 cup Parmesan cheese, shredded

INSTRUCTIONS

1. Chop the thick, woody ends off the asparagus, and discard them. Cut the remaining asparagus into 1" pieces. Set them aside.
2. Add the butter and chopped onion to a pot, and sauté the onions for a few minutes over medium heat.
3. Add the asparagus, and continue sautéing for a few more minutes. Then add the minced garlic and a little salt and pepper, and sauté for 1 minute more.
4. Next, add the chicken broth, and bring it to a boil. Lower the heat, and simmer the asparagus until it is tender (around 10 minutes).
5. Return the soup back to the pot, and add the heavy cream. Cook the soup on medium heat until hot, but do not let it boil.
6. Remove it from the heat, and stir in the shredded Parmesan.
7. Serve and enjoy!

GUACAMOLE

By Maria Jacobson

SERVES: 4–6 | PREP TIME: 15 MINUTES

INGREDIENTS

The Guacamole

1 small bunch cilantro, finely chopped

1 medium red onion, finely diced

1 cup cherry/grape tomatoes, roughly chopped

4 ripe avocados

Juice of 1 lime

½ teaspoon garlic salt

½ teaspoon garlic powder

½ teaspoon onion powder

½ teaspoon black pepper

The Secret Sauce

1–2 tablespoons El Pato Jalapeño! hot sauce (adjusting measurements for more spice)

Tortilla chips, for serving

INSTRUCTIONS

1. Use a festive bowl.
2. Combine the cilantro, onion, and tomatoes in the bowl, and mix well.
3. Add the avocados to the mixture. Mash them to your preferred texture. (We like it chunky!)
4. Squeeze the juice of 1 lime over mixture.
5. Add the seasonings.
6. Add the El Pato Jalapeño! hot sauce. (If you can't find that brand, any jalapeño hot sauce or even minced jalapeños will do.)
7. Fold together all ingredients.
8. Serve the guacamole with tortilla chips and your favorite beverage. Enjoy!

MOROCCAN CHACHOUKA

By Bonnie Sparkman

SERVES: 4–6 | PREP TIME: 5 MINUTES | COOK TIME: 15 MINUTES

INGREDIENTS

2 tablespoons oil
2 cloves garlic, smashed (or to taste)
1 green bell pepper, cut into thin strips
1 28-ounce can tomatoes, whole or diced
¼ teaspoon paprika (more for color than for taste)
Cayenne or chili powder (more or less, depending on how spicy you like it)
Salt, to taste

challah, brioche, crackers, or other crusty bread (for serving)

INSTRUCTIONS

1. Heat the oil over medium heat in a pot. Stir in the garlic and the bell pepper, cooking until the pepper starts getting soft.
2. Add the tomatoes and spices into the pot, and simmer, uncovered, until the tomato juices have cooked off. Use a potato masher to make it less chunky and smoother. The simmering time will be about 15 minutes, depending on how much liquid is released. The chachouka will be a thick consistency when finished. Watch carefully as it thickens, especially at the end, so it does not burn as it cooks down.
3. Serve it cold, warm, or room temperature with challah, brioche, crackers, or other crusty bread for scooping up the salad.

Tip: For extra flavor with no additional time, I use fire-roasted diced tomatoes. I like the Muir Glen brand.

PIRI-PIRI SHRIMP & DIPPING SAUCE

By Pauline Lacroix

SERVES: 4–6 | PREP TIME: 10 MINUTES | COOK TIME: 5 MINUTES

INGREDIENTS

The Shrimp Marinade

1 garlic clove, minced

1 teaspoon cayenne pepper

¼ cup olive oil

2 pounds 16/20 shrimp, peeled and deveined

The Piri-Piri Sauce

4 garlic cloves, minced

½ cup fresh hot red chilies, coarsely chopped

1 teaspoon salt

½ cup olive oil

¼ cup white wine vinegar

Lemon wedges and crusty bread (for serving)

INSTRUCTIONS

The Shrimp

1. Combine the first 3 marinade ingredients, and then add in the shrimp.
2. Cover the shrimp, and marinate it for a minimum of 4 hours in the refrigerator.
3. Cook the marinated shrimp on the BBQ for about 5 minutes (depending on size of shrimps).

The Piri-Piri Dipping Sauce

1. In a food processor or blender, combine the garlic, chilies, salt, olive oil, and white wine vinegar. Process the sauce until well combined.
2. This should yield about 1 cup. You will not use the full cup for the recipe, so you can store the remainder for up to 2 months in the refrigerator.

Serve the shrimp with the dipping sauce, a lemon wedge, and crusty bread.

ROCKET SHRIMP ROLLS

By Dana Contey

YIELD: 36–40 ROLLS | PREP TIME: 40 MINUTES | COOK TIME: 30 MINUTES

INGREDIENTS

1 ½ pounds large shrimp, raw and unpeeled
1 pack spring roll wrappers
7 kaffir lime leaves (fresh or frozen), julienned
2 tablespoons oyster sauce
1 tablespoon sugar
2 teaspoons powdered garlic
¾ teaspoon ground pepper
2 teaspoons sesame oil
1 tablespoon cornstarch
1 egg, beaten (to seal the spring roll wraps)

Optional Toppings

Jufran Banana Sauce (dipping sauce)

Add Sriracha to make the sauce spicier.

INSTRUCTIONS

1. Prep the shrimp: Peel the shrimp, except for the tail, and devein. Score 2 lines on the bottom side of each to straighten the shrimp when frying.
2. Prep the spring roll wrappers: Cut the spring roll wrappers diagonally in half to form 2 triangles. Separate each piece, and keep them in a plastic bag so they don't dry out.
3. Put shrimp in a large mixing bowl, and mix in the kaffir lime leaves, oyster sauce, sugar, powdered garlic, ground pepper, sesame oil, and cornstarch.
4. On a flat surface (cutting board), lay the spring roll wrappers at a 90-degree right angle. Place a shrimp horizontally in the middle of the spring roll wrapper with the shrimp head pointing to the left corner and the tail hanging outside the wrap. Fold the left corner over the shrimp head. Bring the bottom corner over the shrimp so it's lying on top of the top corner. Continue by rolling the shrimp tightly into the top corner of the wrap. Brush a layer of beaten egg to the top corner to seal the spring roll wrap together.
5. Pour 1 ½" to 2" of oil into a skillet, and heat it to 350°F. Add a few rolls to the skillet at a time. Deep fry the shrimp in batches over medium-high heat for 6–8 minutes, turning often, until crisp and golden brown. Drain the rolls on paper towels.
6. Plate and serve the rolls with the dipping sauce, or eat them plain.

SPICY BUFFALO MIXED NUTS

By Rachel Barnett

SERVES: 6–8 | PREP TIME: 5 MINUTES | COOK TIME: 10 MINUTES

INGREDIENTS

2 tablespoons melted butter
¼ cup Frank's RedHot hot sauce
4 teaspoons cayenne powder
½ teaspoon onion powder
½ teaspoon garlic powder
1 teaspoon salt
4 cups mixed nuts
½ teaspoon sea salt

INSTRUCTIONS

1. Preheat the oven to 350°F.
2. Line a baking sheet with a baking mat or parchment paper.
3. In a large bowl, mix the melted butter, Frank's hot sauce, cayenne powder, onion powder, garlic powder, and salt. Stir until well mixed. Add the mixed nuts, and stir until evenly covered.
4. Pour the mixed nuts onto the prepared baking sheet, and spread them into a single layer.
5. Bake the nuts for 5 minutes.
6. Stir the mixed nuts on baking sheet, then sprinkle sea salt on top.
7. Bake the nuts for another 5 minutes.
8. Let them cool before serving.

THAI ROLLS WITH SAKE-LIME DIP

By Pauline Lacroix

YIELD: 5 ROLLS | PREP TIME: 15 MINUTES

INGREDIENTS

The Sake-Lime Dip

¼ cup sake

¼ cup lime juice

1 teaspoon sambal chili paste

3 tablespoons green onion, finely chopped

2 tablespoons granulated sugar

2 tablespoons grapeseed oil

Salt, to taste

The Rolls

1 medium carrot, peeled

1 mango, peeled

1 red pepper

½ English cucumber, peeled

¼ pound rice vermicelli

10 rice paper wrappers

Leaves from ½ bunch Thai basil

INSTRUCTIONS

The Sake-Lime Dip

1. In a bowl, whisk together the sake, lime juice, chili paste, green onion, and sugar.
2. Slowly whisk in the oil until the oil emulsifies.
3. Season the dip with salt, and set it aside.

The Rolls

1. Julienne the vegetables (all the same size), keeping each ingredient separate and putting them into an assembly line.
2. Soak the rice vermicelli in hot water until tender, then drain it.
3. Fill a shallow pan with hot water. Soak 1 rice paper wrapper in the hot water until it is soft and pliable. Place the softened rice paper wrapper on a tea towel, and pat it dry.

(cont'd)

4. Place a small amount of each component (5 of each) plus a few Thai basil leaves on the rice paper. To roll, first taut and fold in the ends, and then tightly roll to form a cigar shape. Cover the rolls with a damp towel.
5. Cut each roll into 2 hors d'oeuvres, and serve them with the dipping sauce.

MAINS

AIR FRYER CHICKEN KATSU

By Lynda Nguyen

SERVES: 3–4 | PREP TIME: 20 MINUTES | COOK TIME: 14 MINUTES

INGREDIENTS

The Katsu Sauce

½ teaspoon sugar
2 tablespoons ketchup
2 tablespoons Worcestershire sauce
1 teaspoon soy sauce

The Chicken

4 boneless, skinless chicken thighs (or 2 chicken breasts, sliced horizontally)
½ teaspoon salt
¼ teaspoon pepper
2 cups panko bread crumbs
1 tablespoon any cooking oil
2 eggs
½ cup all-purpose flour
Olive oil spray

INSTRUCTIONS

The Katsu Sauce

1. Mix together the sugar, ketchup, Worcestershire sauce, and soy sauce in a small bowl. Set it aside to serve with the chicken.

The Chicken

1. Using a meat mallet, place the chicken thighs between layers of plastic wrap or parchment paper, and gently pound it to about ¼" thick. If using chicken breasts, be sure to slice it horizontally first.

(cont'd)

2. Mix the salt and pepper in small bowl, then use it to season both sides of chicken. You can add more seasoning if you'd like. Rest the seasoned chicken on a plate in the fridge while you get the breading station ready.
3. To get that nice golden-brown color, as if we are frying, we will need to toast the panko bread crumbs first. Heat up a pan, and add 1 tablespoon cooking oil. Add the panko bread crumbs, and stir frequently until they turn a light golden brown (approximately 2–3 minutes). Pour the toasted panko crumbs into a bowl.
4. In another bowl, add the two eggs, and whisk gently.
5. Place the flour in a third bowl.
6. Coat the chicken thighs (or breasts) as follows: First, place the chicken in the flour, coating both sides and shaking off the excess. Next, dip the chicken in the egg wash, coating well and shaking off the excess. Finally, place the chicken into the panko, pressing in the bread crumbs to coat well.
7. Lay the coated chicken pieces into an air fryer, lightly spray them with olive oil, and air fry at 380°F for 7 minutes. Flip the pieces over, spray them with some additional olive oil, and cook for another 7 minutes.
8. Transfer the chicken to a plate, slice it, and serve it with katsu sauce over rice or any sides of your choice.

ALBONDIGAS SOUP (MEXICAN MEATBALL SOUP)

By Mia Jones

SERVES: 4–5 | PREP TIME: 45 MINUTES | COOK TIME: 60 MINUTES

INGREDIENTS

The Broth

2 tomatoes (whole)
½ onion, peeled
2 garlic cloves, peeled
1 serrano pepper, stem removed
6 cups water
3 cups chicken broth

The Meatballs

½ cup raw white rice
1 pound ground turkey or ground beef (your choice)
1 egg
½ white onion, finely minced
½ teaspoon dried oregano
Salt, to taste

2 chayote, chopped
4 corn cobbs, halved
3 zucchini squash, chopped
4 large carrots, peeled and chopped

(cont'd)

INSTRUCTIONS

The Broth

1. Place the tomatoes, onion half, garlic cloves, and serrano pepper in a small pot, add just enough water to cover the ingredients, then bring the water to a boil and boil for 5–10 minutes.
2. Once boiled, take the veggies out, transfer them to a blender, and blend.
3. Add 6 cups water and 3 cups chicken broth to a pot, and bring it to a boil.
4. Once the broth comes to a boil, add the blended mixture.

The Meatballs

1. Combine the meatball ingredients with your hands to avoid overmixing.
2. Form fairly large meatballs for even cooking.
3. Once the broth comes to a boil, add the meatballs. They will float to the top when they are cooked.
4. Once all meatballs float to top, add the veggies.
5. Lower the heat, cover the pot with a lid, and simmer the soup until the veggies are tender. Enjoy!

BAKED SWEET-AND-SOUR CHICKEN

By Rachelle Goldhammer

SERVES: 3–4 | PREP TIME: 30 MINUTES | COOK TIME: 60 MINUTES

INGREDIENTS

3–4 boneless chicken breasts
Salt and pepper
1 cup cornstarch
2 eggs, beaten
¼ cup canola oil (plus more for greasing)

¾ cup sugar
¼ cup ketchup
½ cup distilled white vinegar
1 tablespoon soy sauce
1 teaspoon garlic salt

INSTRUCTIONS

1. Preheat the oven to 325°F.
2. Rinse the chicken breasts in water, then cut them into cubes. Season them with salt and pepper to taste. Dip the chicken into the cornstarch to coat, then dip the chicken into the eggs.
3. Heat the oil in a large skillet, then sauté the chicken pieces just until slightly browned but not cooked through.
4. Place the chicken in a greased baking dish.
5. Mix the sugar, ketchup, vinegar, soy sauce, and garlic salt together in a bowl to make the sweet-and-sour sauce. Pour it evenly over the chicken.
6. Bake the chicken for 1 hour, uncovered. During the baking process, turn the chicken every 15 minutes.

BRINED PORK CHOPS WITH SPICY CHUTNEY BARBECUE SAUCE

By Amy Thompson

SERVES: 8 | PREP TIME: 30 MINUTES | COOK TIME: 10 MINUTES

INGREDIENTS

The Brine

8 cups water (divided)

½ cup coarse salt

½ cup packed golden-brown sugar

¼ cup chili powder

8 1 ½"-thick pork chops (bone-in or boneless, your choice)

Oil for grilling

Black pepper, to taste

The Spicy Chutney Barbecue Sauce

2 tablespoons butter

1 medium onion, diced

2 garlic cloves, minced

1 12-ounce bottle chili sauce

1 9- to 10-ounce jar mango chutney

⅓ cup apple cider vinegar

2 tablespoons Worcestershire sauce

2 tablespoons Dijon mustard

1 ½ teaspoons hot pepper sauce

INSTRUCTIONS

The Pork Chops

1. Combine 2 cups of the water with the salt, brown sugar, and chili powder in large, nonreactive pot. Bring the brine to a boil, stirring to dissolve salt and sugar. Remove the brine from heat. Add the remaining 6 cups cold water. Cool the brine completely. Add the pork chops, pressing to submerge. Cover the pot. Chill/brine the pork chops for at least 6 hours or up to 1 day.
2. Preheat the barbecue over medium-high heat.
3. Drain the pork, and pat it dry with paper towels. Brush the pork on both sides with oil, and sprinkle it with black pepper.
4. Grill the pork to desired doneness, about 10 minutes per side or until an instant-read thermometer registers 150°F for medium. Serve the pork with the spicy chutney barbecue sauce.

The Spicy Chutney Barbecue Sauce

1. Melt the butter in a heavy medium saucepan over medium heat.
2. Add the onion, sautéing it until golden, about 5 minutes. Add the garlic, and stir 1 minute.
3. Stir in the chili sauce, chutney, vinegar, Worcestershire sauce, and mustard. Bring the sauce to a boil, then reduce the heat to medium-low, and simmer until the mixture is reduced to 2¾ cups—stirring frequently, about 10 minutes. Stir in the hot pepper sauce.
4. Transfer the sauce to a bowl. Let it cool to room temperature, about 1 hour.

Tip: Prepare the sauce ahead of time. It can be made up to 3 days ahead, covered, and chilled. Bring the sauce to room temperature before serving.

CHICKEN SOUVLAKI

By Pauline Lacroix

SERVES: 8 | PREP TIME: 30 MINUTES | COOK TIME: 13 MINUTES

INGREDIENTS

4 garlic cloves, minced
½ cup lemon juice
½ cup red wine vinegar
2 teaspoons dried oregano
1 teaspoon dried red pepper flakes
5 tablespoons olive oil
1 teaspoon salt
2 teaspoons freshly ground pepper
8 chicken breasts, cubed into 1" pieces
Skewers

INSTRUCTIONS

1. Mix the first 8 ingredients together, then add the chicken. Marinate the chicken for a minimum of 3 hours in the refrigerator.
2. Preheat the barbeque over medium heat. Skewer the marinated chicken and cook on the BBQ for about 13 minutes (depending on size of chicken pieces).

The chicken goes great with Greek lemon rice and Greek salad.

CHICKEN STIR-FRY

By Pauline Lacroix

SERVES: 4 | PREP TIME: 15 MINUTES | COOK TIME: 20 MINUTES

INGREDIENTS

¼ cup grapeseed or coconut oil (divided)
4 boneless, skinless chicken breasts, sliced

1 medium sweet onion
1 red pepper
1 cup broccoli
1 cup cauliflower
1 cup snow peas

6 garlic cloves, minced
½ cup water
6 tablespoons tamari
3 tablespoons rice wine vinegar

3 tablespoons lemongrass, chopped (or use Gourmet Garden Lemongrass Stir-in Paste)
1 cup Thai basil leaves

INSTRUCTIONS

1. Heat half of the oil in a wok or skillet, and cook the chicken until almost done, about 3 minutes. Remove the chicken, and set it aside.
2. Reduce the heat to medium, and add the remaining oil. Add all the vegetables, and cook them till soft, about 4 minutes.
3. Add the garlic, and continue cooking for about 2 minutes. Then add the water, tamari, rice wine vinegar, and chicken. Cook and toss until the chicken is thoroughly cooked, then fold in the lemongrass and Thai basil leaves.
4. Serve the chicken over basmati rice.

CRISPY EGGPLANT AND GOAT CHEESE

By Pauline Lacroix

SERVES: 4 | PREP TIME: 35 MINUTES | COOK TIME: 30 MINUTES

INGREDIENTS

1 Italian eggplant, cut into ½"-thick rounds

Coarse salt

Black pepper, to taste

1 cup panko bread crumbs

½ cup Parmesan cheese, freshly grated

1 cup flour, put in a shallow bowl

4 eggs, beaten

½ cup olive oil

1 cup goat cheese, softened

2 cups marinara sauce

¼ cup fresh basil, chopped

INSTRUCTIONS

1. Sprinkle the sliced eggplant rounds liberally with coarse salt, and then place them in a colander to drain for 30 minutes.
2. Wash the eggplant rounds, pat them dry, and season them with salt and pepper to taste.
3. Combine the panko bread crumbs and Parmesan cheese in a shallow bowl. Coat the eggplant rounds with the flour, followed by eggs, then the bread crumb and Parmesan mixture—patting to adhere.
4. Heat the olive oil in a large frying pan over a medium-high heat, then add the eggplant rounds to pan. Cook the eggplant until golden brown, about 4 minutes per side. Then transfer them to a baking sheet prepared with parchment paper or a baking mat.
5. Spread the goat cheese over half of the eggplant rounds (about 1 tablespoon per round). Stack the remaining rounds on top to form a "sandwich."
6. Bake the rounds until they are heated through and the cheese is melted, about 8 minutes.
7. Serve the eggplant with ½ cup of marina sauce over the top of each round. Sprinkle with fresh basil.

DEEP-DISH PIZZA

By Shawnae McKown

SERVES: 4–6 | PREP TIME: 20–30 MINUTES | COOK TIME: 30–35 MINUTES

INGREDIENTS

The Sauce

1 28-ounce can diced tomatoes
1 8-ounce can tomato sauce
1 6-ounce can tomato paste
½ teaspoon salt
¼ teaspoon garlic powder
¼ teaspoon dried oregano
¼ teaspoon dried basil
¼ teaspoon pepper

Or if you feel lazy like I usually do, you can use any ordinary canned pizza sauce, like Ragu.

The Crust

2 16-ounce bags Trader Joe's Plain Pizza Dough (or you can make homemade dough—but I'm lazy!)
Cooking spray

The Filling

Meats and veggies of your choosing
Mozzarella cheese
Parmesan cheese

INSTRUCTIONS

1. Preheat the oven to 450°F.
2. Combine the sauce ingredients in a medium bowl.
3. Roll out the dough. The base should be about 16". The second dough should be about 12".
4. Spray a 12" deep-dish or spring form pan with cooking spray. Lay the larger dough into the pan so that it covers the bottom and the sides of the pan. Make sure there are no air pockets or holes.
5. Take a small amount of sauce, and rub it on the inside of lid (the top rim).
6. Add the fillings—meats and/or veggies of your choice. (I like to add Canadian bacon, mushrooms, olives, pepperoncini, onion, and bell peppers.)
7. Top the filling with mozzarella cheese—about 1–2 cups or to the top of the pan, depending on how cheesy you want the pizza.
8. Lay the smaller 12" dough on top, and pinch the sides together like a pie. Remove any extra dough. Roll the dough away from the sides. Cut a small hole in the middle of the dough and a few others around the pizza to let steam escape.
9. Add the pizza sauce to the middle, and push it to the outside of pizza until the entire top is covered in a thin layer—but leave the crust along the edge bare.
10. Top the pizza with Parmesan.
11. Bake the pizza for 30–35 minutes.

EAST ROAST CHICKEN

By Bonnie Sparkman

SERVES: 4 | PREP TIME: 10 MINUTES | COOK TIME: 40 MINUTES

INGREDIENTS

The Marinade

2 tablespoons soy sauce
1 tablespoon light brown sugar
2 tablespoons red wine vinegar
3 tablespoons olive oil
4 shallots, chopped
2 cloves garlic, minced
Salt and pepper, to taste

1 whole free-range or corn-fed chicken, broken down into 8 pieces (or 8 of your favorite chicken pieces, preferably skin on and bone in)

Handful of fresh parsley

INSTRUCTIONS

1. Preheat the oven to 425°F.
2. In a large baking dish, combine the marinade ingredients, and toss it with the chicken. Season well with salt and pepper.
3. Place the chicken pieces skin side up, and roast the chicken for 30 minutes, until it begins to brown. Remove it from the oven, and baste the chicken with the pan drippings. Flip the pieces over, and bake the chicken another 10 minutes, or until it is cooked.
4. Garnish the chicken with lots of fresh parsley.

Optional Modifications/Tips

- If your family kids doesn't like vinegar, you can sub it out with teriyaki sauce. The teriyaki flavor is great, but the chicken won't be as crispy as if you had used the vinegar.
- You can also skip the shallots if the kids don't like them. Instead, I pop in some carrots.
- And of course, if you don't have brown sugar, you can use honey. Just make sure it is well mixed in the marinade.
- While you can just put all the ingredients in the baking dish, I choose to put it all in a gallon ziplock bag to make sure the sugar dissolves completely. It also ensures that the chicken gets evenly coated.

If you were wondering, yes, the recipe is correct—you actually don't need to marinate the chicken for any period of time. The chicken can literally go from being mixed with the marinade to the oven. I've tried varying successful marinating times, all depending on the intensity of flavor desired.

INSTANT POT SAUSAGE

By Tracy Cassino

SERVES: 6 | PREP TIME: 15 MINUTES | COOK TIME: 30 MINUTES

INGREDIENTS

2 tablespoons extra-virgin olive oil
1 teaspoon garlic, minced
1 package sweet Italian sausage links (approximately 2 pounds or 14 links)

1 large sweet onion (or 2 medium onions), sliced
3 large red bell peppers, cored and sliced
1 28-ounce can crushed Italian tomatoes (I use San Marzano)
1 15-ounce can tomato sauce
1 teaspoon basil
1 teaspoon thyme
1 teaspoon oregano
½ teaspoon smoked paprika
¼ teaspoon red pepper flakes
1 teaspoon sea salt
½ teaspoon freshly cracked pepper

INSTRUCTIONS

1. With your Instant Pot (IP) on *sauté*, heat the olive oil and add the minced garlic. When the garlic becomes just a little golden in color, add a batch of sausage links. In batches, brown the sausage links on different sides to add color and release flavors. This should take about 5–7 minutes total.
2. When the sausage is done, add the onion, bell peppers, crushed tomatoes, tomato sauce, and the herbs and spices on top. You do *not* need to stir. The IP is going to do its job!

3. Put the IP on *Manual Mode* for 26 minutes. (Adjust the time to suit your preferences; I prefer pork well-done.)
4. When the time is up, do a *Quick Release*.
5. Release the lid, and give the sausages a nice stir to finish melding the flavors together. It will smell and look amazing!

JOLLOF RICE

By Kunle Adetoro

SERVES: 6 | PREP TIME: 30 MINUTES | COOK TIME: 90 MINUTES

INGREDIENTS

6 medium-sized fresh plum/Roma tomatoes, chopped (or a 400-gram tin of tomatoes)
6 fresh red poblano peppers (or 4 large red bell peppers), seeds discarded
3 medium-sized red onions (divided: 1 sliced thinly and 2 roughly chopped)
½ to 1 hot pepper, or to taste (yellow Scotch bonnets are my favorite but they are very spicy!)
5–6 cups vegetable, chicken, or beef stock or water (divided)

⅓ cup oil (vegetable/canola/coconut, not olive oil)
Salt, to taste
2 dried bay leaves
2 teaspoons Caribbean- or Jamaican-style curry powder
1 teaspoon dried thyme
Black and white pepper, to taste
3 tablespoons tomato paste

4 cups uncooked converted long-grain rice or Golden Sella basmati rice, rinsed
2 teaspoons unsalted butter (divided) (optional)
Sliced onions and tomatoes (optional)

INSTRUCTIONS

1. In a blender, combine the plum/Roma tomatoes, red poblano (or bell) peppers, the 2 chopped red onions, and the Scotch bonnet with 1–2 cups of the stock. Blend the mixture till smooth, about a minute or two. You should have roughly 6 cups of blended mix. Pour it into a large pot/pan, and bring it to a boil, then turn down the heat and let it simmer, covered, for 10–12 minutes.
2. In a large pan over medium heat, heat the oil and add the sliced red onion. Season the onion with a pinch of salt, and stir-fry for 2–3 minutes.
3. Then add the bay leaves, curry powder, dried thyme, and a pinch of black pepper. Continue cooking for 3–4 minutes. Then add the tomato paste, and stir for another 2 minutes.
4. Add the reduced tomato, pepper, and Scotch bonnet mixture. Stir, and then continue cooking over medium heat, covered, for 10–12 minutes—till reduced by half. This is the stew that will define the pot.
5. Add the remaining stock (4 cups) to the cooked tomato sauce, and bring it to a boil for 1–2 minutes.
6. Add the rinsed rice and 1 teaspoon of butter (if using). Stir the rice, cover it with a double piece of foil or parchment paper, and put a lid on the pan. This will seal in the steam and lock in the flavor. Turn down the heat, and cook on low for 30 minutes.
7. Stir the rice. Taste for seasoning, and adjust as required.
8. If you like, add sliced onions, fresh tomatoes, and another teaspoon of butter, and stir through.
9. To make "Party Rice," you'll need one more step. Now, Party Rice is essentially smoky Jollof rice, traditionally cooked over an open fire. However, you can achieve the same results on the stove top. Here's how: Once the rice is cooked, turn up the heat with the lid on and leave the rice to "burn" for 3–5 minutes. You'll hear the rice crackle and snap, and it will smell toasted. Turn off the heat, and leave it with the lid on to "rest" till ready to serve. The longer the lid stays on, the smokier the rice will be. Let the party begin!

LEBANESE CHICKEN AND RICE (ROZ A DJEJ)

By Crystal Aboukhaled

SERVES: 6 | PREP TIME: 15 MINUTES | COOK TIME: 60 MINUTES

INGREDIENTS

3 pounds chicken breasts and/or thighs
Salt and freshly ground black pepper, to taste
1 pound ground beef (95 percent lean)
2 tablespoons vegetable, grapeseed, or avocado oil
1 teaspoon ground cinnamon (divided)
3 ¾ teaspoons allspice

3 tablespoons butter
¼ cup rice vermicelli
3 cups white rice
Cooking spray
½ teaspoon nutmeg
2 tablespoons toasted pine nuts or slivered almonds

INSTRUCTIONS

1. In large pot, place the chicken, and add enough water to cover it completely. Season it with salt and pepper, and bring it to a boil. Boil the chicken until it is cooked through, about 30 minutes.
2. While the chicken is boiling, heat a large pan or skillet with the oil over medium-high heat. Add the ground beef, breaking it up with a spoon and cooking it until browned. Add a ½ teaspoon of the cinnamon to the beef while it is cooking.
3. Once the chicken is cooked, remove it from the broth to let it cool. Reserve the broth to cook the rice. Cut/shred the chicken into large chunks. Season the chicken with salt and pepper (to taste), the allspice, and the remaining cinnamon—enough spice to coat the pieces of chicken.
4. In a large pot, add the butter over medium-high heat. Then add the rice vermicelli, and sauté it until browned.
5. Add the rice to the large pot with the vermicelli, stirring to combine the butter, rice, and vermicelli.
6. Once the rice and vermicelli are combined, add 3 cups of the reserved chicken broth.
7. Bring to the rice to a boil, then reduce the heat and simmer for 15 minutes, or until the broth is absorbed. Fluff the rice with a fork.
8. Spray a large baking dish with cooking spray, and preheat the oven to 350°F.
9. Combine the chicken, rice, and ground beef (either directly in the baking dish or separately in a large bowl before being transferred to the baking dish). Add the nutmeg and additional allspice (to taste).
10. Cover the dish with foil, and bake it for 15–20 minutes until heated through.
11. Optional: sauté pine nuts or slivered almonds with oil until the nuts are golden brown, about 2–3 minutes.
12. Once the rice is heated through, empty it onto a serving platter, and top it with the nuts.

(cont'd)

Notes

- Any chicken can be used—whole chicken, breasts, or thighs. Boneless and skinless is preferred. If you are short on time, pick up a rotisserie chicken!
- Basmati rice works wonderfully in this recipe, as would any other long-grain rice.
- Rice vermicelli is a very fine noodle—sold in Asian markets and the Asian-food section of supermarkets—but it can be omitted if needed.
- Seasoning is subjective, so measure with your heart with all the spices, salt, and pepper.

LOUISIANA GUMBO

By Blair Gavitt

SERVES: 4 | PREP TIME: 30 MINUTES | COOK TIME: 60 MINUTES

INGREDIENTS

2 cups onions, chopped
1 ½ cups green bell peppers, chopped
1 cups celery, chopped

2 bay leaves
2 teaspoons salt
½ teaspoon white pepper
½ teaspoon cayenne pepper
½ teaspoon black pepper
½ teaspoon dried thyme
½ teaspoon dried oregano

¾ cup vegetable oil
¾ cup all-purpose flour (substitute rice flour for a gluten-free option)
1 tablespoon garlic, minced or pressed

5 ½ cups seafood stock
1 pound andouille, cut into ½" pieces
1 pound medium shrimp, peeled
¾ pound crab meat, picked over
2 ½ cups hot cooked rice

(cont'd)

INSTRUCTIONS

1. Combine the onions, bell peppers, and celery in a medium-size bowl, and set it aside. In a small bowl, combine the next 7 ingredients for seasoning; mix it well, and set it aside.
2. Heat the oil in a large skillet over high heat until it starts to smoke, about
   5 minutes.
3. Gradually add the flour to the oil to form a roux, whisking constantly with a metal whisk. Continue cooking and whisking until the roux is dark red/brown to black, 2–4 minutes.
4. Immediately add half the vegetable mirepoix (onions, peppers, and celery), and stir well for 1 minutes, switching to a spoon if necessary.
5. Add the remaining vegetables, continuing to stir about 2 minutes. Add the seasoning mix, and continue to cook about 2 minutes.
6. Add the garlic, stirring well for another minute. Remove the skillet from heat.
7. Place the stock in a 5 ½-quart saucepan or Dutch oven, and bring it to a boil. Add the roux mixture by spoonful, stirring until the roux is dissolved in between each addition. Bring the stock back to a boil.
8. Add the andouille, and return the stock to a boil again. Continue boiling for 15 minutes, stirring occasionally. Reduce the heat, and simmer the andouille 10 minutes.
9. Add the shrimp and crab meat. Return the stock to a boil, stirring occasionally.
10. Remove the gumbo from the heat, skim oil from the surface, and serve it over the rice.

MARINARA SAUCE

By Pauline Lacroix

YIELD: 4 CUPS | PREP TIME: 10 MINUTES | COOK TIME: 50 MINUTES

INGREDIENTS

¼ cup olive oil
2 medium onions, finely diced
4 garlic cloves, minced
¼ cup dry white wine (optional)
2 28-ounce cans plum tomatoes
2 teaspoons fresh oregano or ¼ teaspoon dried oregano, crumbled
½ teaspoon sugar
2 tablespoons fresh basil, hand torn
Salt and pepper, to taste

INSTRUCTIONS

1. Heat the olive oil in a large saucepan over medium heat.
2. Add the onions and garlic, and sauté them until translucent, about 7 minutes.
3. Add the wine (if using), and cook about 1 minute.
4. Add the tomatoes, oregano, and sugar. Simmer until the sauce has thickened, stirring occasionally, about 45 minutes.
5. Season with salt and pepper, and add the fresh basil.

This marinara sauce is great with the "Crispy Eggplant and Goat Cheese" recipe on page 50...and a chilled crisp white wine.

SCOTT JUREK'S MINNESOTA WINTER CHILI (VEGAN)

By Angel Cushma

SERVES: 8–10 | PREP TIME: 30 MINUTES | COOK TIME: 60 MINUTES

INGREDIENTS

2 tablespoons coconut oil or olive oil
2 garlic cloves, minced
1 cup onion, finely chopped
8–10 medium mushrooms, finely chopped
½ cup green bell pepper, finely chopped
½ cup red bell pepper, finely chopped
½ cup carrots, finely chopped
1 jalapeño pepper or other hot pepper, seeded and minced (optional)
1 cup frozen corn kernels
1 teaspoon ground cumin
½ teaspoon ground coriander
2 tablespoons chili powder
2 teaspoons sea salt, plus more to taste
½ teaspoon black pepper

1 28-ounce can diced tomatoes
1 15-ounce can tomato puree
1 15-ounce can kidney beans, drained
1 15-ounce can black beans, drained
1 15-ounce can red beans, drained
2 ½ cups water
½ cup dry bulgur wheat
Hot sauce or cayenne pepper (optional)
¼ cup fresh cilantro, minced (for garnish)

INSTRUCTIONS

1. Add the oil to a large pot. Sauté the vegetables and spices in the oil over medium to medium-low heat for 10 minutes or until tender. Add a few tablespoons of water if the veggies begin sticking to the pot.
2. Add the remaining ingredients, except the cilantro, and simmer the chili over medium-low heat, covered, for 30 minutes. Stir and simmer for an additional 20–30 minutes, or until the veggies are cooked through.
3. Season with salt and, if more spice is desired, additional hot sauce or cayenne pepper to taste. Serve the chili sprinkled with the cilantro.
4. You can also just put all the ingredients in a Crock-Pot, after sautéing the vegetables, and cook the chili on high for about 4 hours or low for 8 hours.

OSSO BUCO

By Pauline Lacroix

SERVES: 4 | PREP TIME: 20 MINUTES | COOK TIME: 2 ½ HOURS

INGREDIENTS

The Osso Buco

2 tablespoons olive oil
4 thick veal shanks
Salt and pepper, to taste
¼ cup flour
1 onion, finely diced
2 garlic cloves, minced
½ cup dry red wine
1 28-ounce can diced plum tomatoes
2 cups chicken stock
2 tablespoons fresh rosemary, chopped

The Gremolata

2 tablespoons fresh parsley, minced
2 garlic cloves, minced
1 teaspoon lemon zest, grated
½ teaspoon black pepper, cracked

INSTRUCTIONS

1. Heat the olive oil in a 3-quart pot over medium-high heat.
2. Season the veal shanks with salt and pepper, and dredge them in the flour, shaking off the excess. Add the veal shanks to the pot. Cook until deep golden brown, turning once (a total of about 12 minutes). Transfer the veal shanks to a bowl.
3. Reduce the heat to medium-low. Add the onion and garlic, and sauté them until tender (about 5 minutes). Add more olive oil if needed.
4. Deglaze the onions with the wine, and reduce the wine by half.
5. Add the diced tomatoes, chicken stock, and rosemary to the pot, stir, then add the veal shanks and any juices from the bowl. Partially cover the pot, and simmer the veal shanks until they are tender and the meat begins to fall off the bones, about 2 ½ hours.
6. Meanwhile, combine the gremolata ingredients in a small bowl, and set it aside.
7. To serve, ladle one veal shank into a shallow bowl with a bit of sauce and a sprinkle of the gremolata on top.

The osso buco goes great with mashed potatoes or risotto Milanese.

PERSIAN CHICKEN KABOB (JUJEH KABOB)

By Darius Goodall

SERVES: 4 | PREP TIME: 15 MINUTES | MARINATION TIME: 24 HOURS | COOK TIME: 15 MINUTES

INGREDIENTS

The Marinade

1 teaspoon saffron threads

2 teaspoons salt (divided)

1 tablespoon boiling water

½ cup olive oil

2 teaspoons black pepper, freshly cracked

1 cup lime juice, freshly squeezed

2 large onions (red onions provide more flavor, but white are OK too)

3 pounds chicken thighs, trimmed and halved

For Basting

½ stick butter, melted

3 tablespoons lime juice, freshly squeezed

½ teaspoon salt

½ teaspoon black pepper, freshly cracked

INSTRUCTIONS

1. In a small mortar and pestle, add the saffron threads and a ½ teaspoon of the salt. Grind them to a powder. Add about 1 tablespoon of boiling water to dissolve the salt and turn the saffron into a "saffron tea."
2. In a large mixing bowl, add the olive oil, remaining 1 ½ teaspoons salt, black pepper, lime juice, and saffron tea. Mix the marinade well, and set it aside.

3. Halve and then thinly slice the onions, and add them to the mixing bowl to create an intense yet fragrant marinade.
4. Trim the chicken thighs of fat, halve them, and add them to the marinade. Mix well, getting a good coating of the marinade over the chicken. Cover the chicken with plastic wrap, and place it in the fridge for 24 hours.

To Cook

1. Persian chicken kabob (jujeh kabob) is traditionally cooked over charcoal or a burned-down wood fire. This adds wonderfully sophisticated smoky notes to the meal. If you cannot cook over a charcoal or wood fire, simply grilling or broiling the kabobs works too.
2. Half an hour prior to cooking, start a good, strong fire that will last.
3. If you have skewers/swords, skewer the meat, folding each thigh in half on the skewer. If not, you'll be grilling the individual thighs over the fire, which is fine, too, but somewhat less impressive visually. The swords do help cook the meat from the inside out too.

(cont'd)

4. Once the fire is ready, place the skewers over the heat, positioning them so that the chicken will cook in about 15 minutes. You're looking for a slight char, which adds color and texture to the meat.
5. Combine the basting ingredients in a small bowl, and baste the chicken with the basting mixture regularly. Do not allow the meat to dry; it should always be wet with the basting mixture.
6. While the chicken is grilling, take the rest of the contents of the mixing bowl (the remaining marinated onions and juice) and fry them until the liquid is all gone and the onions are just starting to brown.
7. Serve and enjoy.

Persian chicken kabobs are traditionally served with lavash bread, fluffy white basmati rice, raw onion (trust me, this is actually really good—you have to try it), pomegranate seeds, skewered and grilled plum tomatoes, mint leaves, cilantro, butter, lime, feta cheese, and ground sumac. Take a bit of everything, place it on a quarter sheet of lavash bread, and fold it into a Persian taco. Enjoy!

PUMPKIN-SAGE ALFREDO

By Sheryl Howley Johnson

SERVES: 4 | PREP TIME: 30 MINUTES | COOK TIME: 60 MINUTES

INGREDIENTS

Homemade Pumpkin-Sage Pasta

(Or substitute 1 pound store-bought pasta)

A pinch ground turmeric (optional, for deeper color)
A few sage leaves, finely minced (optional)
2 cups flour
2 eggs
¼ cup pumpkin puree

The Creamy Pumpkin-Sage Sauce

1 cup pumpkin puree (about half a small roasted pumpkin)
¾ cup half-and-half
¼ cup butter
1 tablespoon fresh sage, minced
Salt and black pepper, to taste

Sage Chips (Optional Garnish)

¼ cup grapeseed oil
12 fresh sage leaves
Pinch of salt

4 quarts water
1 tablespoon salt
½ cup Parmesan, grated
Grated nutmeg, to taste

(cont'd)

INSTRUCTIONS

1. You can make the pasta by hand, or you can use a food processor if you prefer. In a small bowl, whisk the turmeric and sage into the flour. Pour the flour onto a clean surface, heaped in a mound, and use your hand to make an indentation in the middle. Crack the two eggs into this hollow space, and add the pumpkin puree as well. Blend the eggs and pumpkin with a fork, slowly incorporating them into the flour and pushing in more flour with your other hand. As the dough starts to come together, use your hands to gradually begin to shape it into a rough ball, collecting all the remaining flour as you go. Knead the dough for a few minutes until it becomes smooth. If the dough is too dry, add a tiny bit of water, half a teaspoon at a time. The dough should feel a little sticky; however, bits of dough should not be sticking to your hands or the countertop. If it is too sticky, add a little flour (a tablespoon at a time), continuing to knead between each addition. Cover the dough with a damp, clean cloth, and allow the dough to rest for about 30 minutes.
2. After 30 minutes, cut the ball into 8 pieces. Dust a clean surface with a generous amount of flour, and use a rolling pin (or a pasta maker) to roll each piece of dough as thinly as you can, into a long rectangular shape. Continually dust the rolled dough with flour to make sure it doesn't stick. Using a pizza cutter or sharp knife, cut the dough into fettuccine-sized strips. Dust the strips with flour again to prevent the noodles from sticking, and lay them on a baking sheet until you are ready to cook them.
3. To make the sauce, mix the pumpkin purée and half-and-half together using a blender or hand blender. In a large skillet, melt the butter and minced sage over low heat. Add the pumpkin and cream puree to the sage butter, and stir. Bring the sauce to barely a simmer, and turn off the heat. Add salt and pepper to taste. Place the sauce aside until the pasta has been boiled.

4. To make the sage chips, pour the oil in a small skillet or saucepan, and place it over medium heat. The oil is hot enough when a sage leaf dropped in starts to sizzle right away. Fry a few sage leaves at a time, just until crispy. It takes about 15 seconds, depending on how hot the oil is. Do not let them burn or turn brown. Remove the sage from the hot oil, and place them on a paper towel. Sprinkle them with salt.
5. Meanwhile, bring a large pot of about 4 quarts of water to a boil. Add a tablespoon of salt and the pasta to the boiling water. Stir the pasta gently to prevent it from sticking together. Cook for about 1 minute. Place the pumpkin-sage sauce back on medium-low heat, and bring the pot of pasta close to the skillet. Using tongs, quickly remove the pasta from the water, transferring it directly into the pumpkin sauce. You do not need to drain the pasta, a little water in the sauce is fine. Add all but a tablespoon of the grated Parmesan, and cook over low heat for 1–2 more minutes, until the sauce has thickened and the pasta is cooked to your liking. Do not overcook the pasta, or it will get mushy. Serve the pasta immediately, and top it with the rest of the grated Parmesan, a little grated nutmeg, and the sage chips.

QUINOA SALAD WITH JALAPEÑO-LIME VINAIGRETTE

By Deanna Brownley

SERVES: 4–6 | PREP TIME: 40 MINUTES

INGREDIENTS

Kosher salt
1 cup quinoa
1 garlic clove, pounded to a smooth paste with a pinch of salt
1 large shallot, finely diced (or omit and triple the garlic)
1 jalapeño, seeded and finely diced (⅛" dice)
3 ½ tablespoons lime juice, freshly squeezed (plus more as needed, to taste)
Salt, to taste
½ cup plus 2 tablespoons high-quality extra-virgin olive oil
1 medium red pepper, halved, seeded, and cut into ¼" dice
1 small-to-medium cucumber, peeled, seeded, and cut into ¼" dice (about 1 cup)
½ cup fresh cilantro, roughly chopped (plus sprigs for garnish)
2–3 ripe avocados, sliced

INSTRUCTIONS

1. Bring a large pot of water to a boil, and generously season it with salt. Rinse the quinoa under cool running water, lightly rubbing it between your fingers for a few seconds. Add it to the boiling water, and cook it until tender, 12–15 minutes. (Al dente is OK, as the quinoa will absorb some of the vinaigrette.)
2. Drain the quinoa well with a fine sieve, and spread it out on a baking sheet to cool/dry. This step is important: if the quinoa is too wet, it will water down the flavor of the vinaigrette; if it is still hot, it can cook the veggies, and they will lose their crunch.

3. While the quinoa is cooking/cooling, prep the vinaigrette and vegetables. Put the garlic, shallot, jalapeño, and lime juice in a small bowl. Season the mixture with salt, and stir to combine. Let it sit for 5–10 minutes. Add ½ cup of the oil, and whisk to combine. Taste for seasoning, and add more salt or lime juice if needed.
4. Put the quinoa, red pepper, cucumber, and chopped cilantro in a medium bowl. Drizzle about half of the vinaigrette into the bowl, and gently fold it in to combine. Taste for seasoning, and add more salt, vinaigrette, and/or lime juice as needed.
5. Arrange the sliced avocados on a platter or individual serving plates. Season the avocado with salt, and drizzle the remaining vinaigrette on top. Spoon the quinoa salad on and around the avocado. Garnish with the cilantro sprigs, and serve.

Notes

- You can serve the salad as is or with a couple of variations. Variation 1: cut the avocado into chunks, fold it right into salad, and serve. (The lime juice in the vinaigrette will keep it from turning brown.) Variation 2: cut the avocado into chunks, fold it into salad, and serve the salad in red lettuce or green lettuce cups, individual-sized. I add cotija cheese on top when serving the salad as lettuce cups.
- You can also add grilled, shredded chicken (or your protein of choice) to create a main course. Enjoy!

RAVIOLI LASAGNA

By Heather Andrews

SERVES: 6 | PREP TIME: 10 MINUTES | COOK TIME: 30 MINUTES

INGREDIENTS

1 tablespoon olive oil (plus 1 teaspoon to grease the pan)
1 pound spicy Italian sausage, casings removed
2 24-ounce jars marinara sauce
2 pounds frozen cheese ravioli, thawed (about 24 ravioli)
2 ½ cups shredded mozzarella cheese
1 cup Parmesan cheese, freshly grated

INSTRUCTIONS

1. Preheat the oven to 400°F.
2. Brush a 9" × 13" pan with 1 teaspoon of the olive oil.
3. Heat a large skillet over medium heat. Add the remaining 1 tablespoon olive oil and the sausage (or ground turkey). (Note: I add Italian seasoning, garlic salt, pepper, and oregano to my ground turkey.) Cook, breaking up the sausage into bite-sized pieces with the back of a wooden spoon, until the sausage is beginning to brown, about 8 minutes. Add the marinara, and bring it to a simmer. Remove the sauce from the heat, and let it cool slightly.
4. Spoon a third of the sauce mixture over the bottom of the pan.
5. Place a layer of ravioli on top of the sauce.
6. Spoon half of the remaining sauce on top of the ravioli.
7. Sprinkle the sauce with 1 cup of the mozzarella and ½ cup of the Parmesan.
8. Repeat with another layer of ravioli.

9. Top with the remaining sauce, mozzarella, and Parmesan.
10. Place the lasagna in the oven, and bake it for 25 minutes or until bubbling around the edges.
11. Switch the oven to broil, and broil the lasagna on high for 3–4 minutes or until the cheese is golden brown.
12. Allow the lasagna to sit for 10 minutes before serving. Enjoy!

Tips

For a healthier, milder version, substitute ground turkey for the sausage

SEAFOOD CHOWDER

By Krystan Bugbee

SERVES: 24 | PREP TIME: 30 MINUTES | COOK TIME: 3½ HOURS

INGREDIENTS

¼ pound salt pork, cut into three strips
12 large Idaho baking potatoes
1 large onion, chopped
½ cup clams, minced (8 large, 12 medium, or 15 small clams; or 1 small can of minced clams)
1 ½ teaspoons salt
1 teaspoon pepper
2 ½ sticks butter
2 bay leaves
8 pounds fresh haddock (boneless, skinless), cut into 6" pieces
1 ½ pounds freshly cooked lobster meat
1 ½ quarts light cream
Parsley (optional, for garnish)
Oyster crackers (optional)

INSTRUCTIONS

1. Place the salt pork strips in a stockpot on low heat.
2. Peel and wash the potatoes, then cut them into ½" to ¾" pieces. Place them in the stockpot, and cover them evenly with cold water. (Do not place more than ½" of water over the potatoes.)
3. Add the onion, minced clams, salt, pepper, 1 stick of the butter, and bay leaves to the pot. Bring it to a boil, then turn the heat down and simmer it for 2 ½ hours.
4. Place the haddock pieces on top of the chowder.
5. Add 1 ½ sticks of butter, then turn the heat to medium. Cook the chowder until the fish is soft enough to break apart with a wooden spoon (approximately 45 minutes).
6. Remove the salt pork and bay leaves.
7. Add the lobster meat and light cream. Stir well and simmer on low heat approximately 20 minutes, until the butter is melted.
8. Garnish with parsley if desired. Serve hot with oyster crackers.

SPAM FRIED RICE

By Laura Lee

SERVES: 2 | PREP TIME: 5 MINUTES | COOK TIME: 10 MINUTES

INGREDIENTS

½ small white onion

½ stalk green onion (green part only)

6 ounces Spam

1 10-ounce bag frozen cauliflower rice

1 ½ tablespoons sesame oil (divided)

1 egg

Soy sauce, to taste

Salt and pepper, to taste

INSTRUCTIONS

1. Finely dice the onion and green onion top, and set them aside.
2. Cube the Spam into small bite-size pieces, and set it aside.
3. Microwave the cauliflower until it is not frozen, about 2 minutes, and set it aside.
4. Heat 1 tablespoon of the sesame oil on high heat in a skillet, then add the Spam. Cook it for 3–4 minutes until it is browned, then remove it from the pan.
5. Add the white onion to the pan, and cook it for 2–3 minutes. Then add the cauliflower, and cook it with the onion for 3–4 more minutes.
6. Make a large hole in the middle of the "rice," and add ½ tablespoon sesame oil and 1 egg.
7. Scrambled the egg, and mix it into the rice.
8. Add the green onion, soy sauce, and salt and pepper to taste. Serve and enjoy!

SPICY FUSILLI

By Ashleigh Hookano

SERVES: 2 | PREP TIME: 10 MINUTES | COOK TIME: 20 MINUTES

INGREDIENTS

2 garlic cloves (or more, depending on your love for garlic!)
1 shallot
Salt (for the pasta water)
¼ cup olive oil
½ cup tomato paste
2 tablespoons vodka
1 ¾ cups heavy cream (divided)
½ tablespoon red pepper flakes
Salt and pepper, to taste
½ pound fusilli
½ cup butter
½ cup Parmesan

Optional Toppings/Sides
Basil leaves
Garlic bread
Side salad

INSTRUCTIONS

Prep

1. Chop the garlic and shallot.
2. Bring a pot of water to a boil, and salt it.

The Sauce

1. Heat the olive oil in a pan over medium-low heat. Add the chopped garlic and shallot, and cook them until browned.
2. Stir in the tomato paste, and cook it for about 5 minutes, until it turns a dark reddish-brown.
3. Add the vodka, then 1 ¼ cups of the heavy cream, and cook for about 2 or 3 minutes.
4. Season the sauce with the red pepper flakes and salt to taste.

The Pasta

1. When the water is boiling, cook the fusilli until al dente (per the instructions on the box).
2. Strain the pasta, and reserve about 1 cup of the pasta water.
3. Add the remaining ½ cup heavy cream and the butter to the sauce.
4. Add the cooked pasta to the sauce, and toss it.
5. Slowly add in the pasta water to thin the sauce. This step is up to you—add as much as feels right! I usually use a little over ½ cup. Don't thin out the sauce too much.
6. Add in the Parmesan. Stir until the Parmesan has melted and the sauce and pasta are fully combined.
7. Top with the basil (if using). Add salt and pepper to taste.
8. Serve with garlic bread and a side salad (optional).

SPICY SALT-AND-PEPPER PORK CHOP

By Regina Gruezo

SERVES: 6–8 | PREP TIME: 20 MINUTES | COOK TIME: 15 MINUTES

INGREDIENTS

8–10 pork chops, thinly sliced
1 tablespoon salt
1 tablespoon cayenne pepper
1 tablespoon garlic powder
1 tablespoon soy sauce
1 tablespoon sesame oil
¼ teaspoon baking soda
2 cups tapioca flour
1 ½ tablespoons cooking oil
6 garlic cloves, diced
2 large jalapeño or serrano peppers, thinly sliced (about ⅛")
3 stalks green onion, thinly sliced (about ⅛")

INSTRUCTIONS

1. Cut the pork chops into 3 pieces (1" width).
2. Mix the pork chops with the salt, cayenne pepper, garlic powder, soy sauce, sesame oil, and baking soda. Marinate them for 15 minutes.
3. Before frying the pork chops, coat each pork chop completely with tapioca flour.
4. Heat a large pan, and add the cooking oil. Fry the pork chops until browned. Remove them, and set them aside.
5. Add the diced garlic to the pan, and sauté it until it has slightly browned. Add the sliced jalapeño/serrano peppers and the sliced green onion.
6. Add the fried pork chops, and coat them with the garlic topping.
7. Finish with seasoned salt and/or cayenne pepper. The pork chops are best when served hot and crispy.

STEAK AND KIDNEY PIE

By Pauline Lacroix

SERVES: 6 | PREP TIME: 30 MINUTES | COOK TIME: 2 HOURS

INGREDIENTS

2 tablespoons olive oil
2 tablespoons butter
1 large onion
1 ½ pounds of chuck or ribeye steak, cut into 1" pieces
2 tablespoons flour
5 ounces of lamb kidneys, diced
3 cups beef stock
1 ¼ teaspoons Dijon mustard
1 bay leaf
Salt and pepper, to taste
3 dashes of Worcestershire sauce (or to taste)
1 sheet puff pastry
1 egg, beaten

INSTRUCTIONS

1. Heat a fry pan, then add the oil, butter, and onions. Fry the onions till they are soft and translucent.
2. Add the steak, and cook it till it is slightly browned.
3. Stir in the flour, and allow the mixture to cook for a few minutes, then add the kidneys and cook them for 1 or 2 minutes longer.
4. Add the beef stock, mustard, bay leaf, salt, pepper, and Worcestershire sauce to the meat and onions. Simmer the stew uncovered for 90 minutes, stirring occasionally. If the mixture becomes too dry, add a little more beef stock.
5. Remove the stew from the heat, and allow it to completely cool.

6. Preheat the oven to 425°F
7. Scoop the cooled stew into a pie pan.
8. Place the puff pastry on top of the pie pan, and then trim and crimp the edges.
9. Cut small slits in the middle of the pastry.
10. Brush the top of pastry with the beaten egg.
11. Bake the pie for 30 minutes until the pastry is golden.

SUPER EASY WEEKNIGHT CHICKEN

By Michelle Coulombe

SERVES: 1 | PREP TIME: 10 MINUTES | COOK TIME: 15 MINUTES

INGREDIENTS

3 chicken breasts, boneless
Salt and pepper, to taste
Oil (for greasing the baking dish)
½ cup mayonnaise
½ cup Parmesan cheese, grated
1 teaspoon Italian seasoning mix (Mrs. Dash version is my personal favorite.)
1 clove garlic, pressed or finely minced

Substitutions/Variations

Rosemary herb blend instead of Italian seasoning
Mexican spice blend and finely shredded Mexican cheese blend instead of Italian seasoning and Parmesan

---

INSTRUCTIONS

1. Preheat the oven to 425°F.
2. Split the chicken breasts lengthwise. Lightly salt and pepper both sides of the chicken, and arrange them on a lightly oiled baking dish.
3. In a small bowl, mix the mayonnaise, Parmesan cheese, herb blend, and garlic.
4. Top each of the six pieces of chicken with an even amount of the mayo blend, spread evenly.
5. Bake the chicken for 15–20 minutes.

Yup! That's it! The perfect solution when you don't know what the heck you're going to do with another package of chicken breasts. I serve the chicken with thinly sliced, roasted delicata squash and rice or couscous.

TACO SOUP

By Joe Felz

SERVES: 6 | PREP TIME: 10 MINUTES | COOK TIME: 4 HOURS

INGREDIENTS

1 pound hamburger, 90 percent lean (or ground turkey)
Minced onions, black pepper, and cayenne pepper, to taste
1 10-ounce can Ro*Tel Original Diced Tomatoes & Green Chilies
1 15-ounce can pinto beans
1 15-ounce can black beans
1 15-ounce can chili beans
1 15-ounce can yellow corn
1 package Taco Bell seasoning mix (or another brand of taco seasoning)
1 package Hidden Valley Ranch dip mix (or another brand of ranch dip mix)

To Serve

Grated cheese; tortilla strips/chips/scoops

INSTRUCTIONS

1. Spray the inside of a Crock-Pot with cooking spray.
2. In a skillet, brown the hamburger, minced onions, black pepper, and cayenne pepper. Once browned, transfer the hamburger into the Crock-Pot.
3. Add all the other ingredients. Don't drain the beans and corn.
4. Add 15 ounces of water, and mix the ingredients together.
5. Cook the soup all day on low or 4 hours on high. If you want to eat sooner, you can cook the soup in a big pot on the stove for 1 hour instead of in a Crock-Pot.
6. To serve, top the soup with the grated cheese and tortilla strips. It's great with tortilla chips or scoops to dip!

THAI GREEN CURRY (GAENG KEOW WAN)

By Bonnie Sparkman

SERVES: 1 | PREP TIME: 15 MINUTES | COOK TIME: 7 MINUTES

INGREDIENTS

Green Curry Paste

20 Thai green chilies (if you'd like the curry to be spicy), adjust to taste
1 teaspoon minced galangal
3 tablespoons minced lemongrass
3 Kaffir lime leaves, finely sliced
2 tablespoons minced garlic
3 tablespoons minced shallots
1 teaspoon salt
1 handful Thai sweet basil leaves, to taste
2 tablespoons vegetable oil

Green Curry with Meat of Your Choice

1 tablespoon vegetable oil
1 tablespoon green curry paste (see above), or to taste
1 handful of the meat of your choice (or vegetables), sliced into bite-size pieces
¾ cup plus a few tablespoons coconut milk
2 tablespoons fish sauce
1 tablespoon sugar
200 ml chicken stock or water
1 handful green beans, cut into 1" pieces
1 handful bamboo shoots
2 Kaffir lime leaves
Jasmine rice (for serving

INSTRUCTIONS

Green Curry Paste

1. Using a mortar and pestle, mash all the ingredients except for the oil.
2. Stir in the oil last to make a smooth paste.

Tip: Depending on how big your mortar is, instead of using your hand as a guard, you can also cover the mortar with plastic wrap. This reduces the risk of getting the chili liquid in your eyes.

Green Curry with Meat of Your Choice

1. In a pot over low heat, mix well the oil and green curry paste.
2. Then add the meat (or vegetables, for vegetarians). Stir until all is half-cooked.
3. Add the coconut milk, fish sauce, and sugar. Mix well.
4. Add the chicken stock, green beans, and bamboo shoots
5. Bring the curry to a boil, then immediately pour it into a serving bowl, and garnish it with the kaffir lime leaves.
6. Serve the curry with jasmine rice.

THE DINER'S CHICKEN ENCHILADAS

By Meg Gleeson

SERVES: 4–6 | PREP TIME: 15 MINUTES | COOK TIME: 45 MINUTES

INGREDIENTS

The Filling

2 cups cooked chicken breast, shredded into bite-size pieces
2 ½ cups Monterey Jack cheese, coarsely grated and loosely packed (about 8 ounces)
½ cup red onion, chopped
1 12-ounce package 7" flour tortillas (10 tortillas)

The Sauce

2 tablespoons butter
2 tablespoons flour
2 cups low-sodium chicken broth
1 ½ cups sour cream
2 4-ounce cans diced green chilies (mild or hot or a combo)

Toppings

½ cup scallions, chopped

INSTRUCTIONS

1. Preheat the oven to 350°F.

Make the Filling

1. In medium-sized bowl, mix the chicken, 1 ½ cups of the Monterey Jack cheese, and the red onion.
2. Place ½ cup of the mixture on the bottom half of each tortilla, and roll them up. Arrange the rolled tortillas, seam side down, in a 13" × 9" × 2" baking dish, and set them aside.

Make the Sauce

1. Melt the butter in heavy 2-quart saucepan over low heat. Sprinkle in the flour, stirring constantly for 5 full minutes. Add the chicken broth, continuing to stir. Increase the heat to medium, stirring about 3 more minutes until mixture begins to bubble and thicken. Remove the broth from the heat.
2. Fold in the sour cream and green chilies.
3. Pour the sauce over the rolled tortillas in the baking dish. Then bake the enchiladas, uncovered, for 30 minutes.
4. Sprinkle the enchiladas with the remaining 1 cup of the Monterey Jack cheese and the scallions. Bake them for 15 minutes longer or until the cheese has melted.

Side Dish Suggestions

- Black beans sprinkled with cotija cheese
- Cabbage slaw with cilantro and vinaigrette
- Chips, guacamole, and salsa

TONNINO SPAGHETTI MEDITERRANEAN-STYLE

By Kathleen Krasniqi

SERVES: 5 | PREP TIME: 10 MINUTES | COOK TIME: 20 MINUTES

INGREDIENTS

1 pound thick spaghetti (such as Barilla)
2 cloves garlic, diced
¾ cup olive oil
1 jar Tonnino tuna fillets (in a glass jar, not canned!), drained
You can use Tonnino tuna that comes packed in oil or water. I prefer it in water, and I drain the water out before frying.
Several Fefferoni yellow peppers (mild or spicy), chopped, to taste
A handful of feta cheese (packed in water), drained and crumbled
Salt and pepper, to taste

INSTRUCTIONS

1. Dice fresh garlic. For a box of spaghetti, you should use at least 2 cloves of garlic.
2. Dice Fefferoni, mild or spicey, use about 3 to give it flavor or as much as you prefer.
3. Add about ¾ cup of Olive Oil in a pan and simmer low.
4. Prepare the spaghetti according to the package instructions.
5. As the spaghetti boils, take your pan with hot olive oil and sauté your garlic and fefferoni.
6. Add one teaspoon of salt sprinkled over your sautéed garlic and fefferoni, continue sauteing for a few minutes.
7. Add the Tonnino tuna mixing as it is added. Sautee lightly, just enough to warm the tuna. Don't let the garlic brown.
8. Once done, drain the pasta and add to a large pasta serving bowl
9. Pour the olive oil, garlic, fefferoni, and Tonnino Tuna mixture over the pasta
10. Sprinkle feta cheese on the dish
11. Enjoy the spaghetti with a glass of wine!

VEGETABLE-PASTA BAKE

By Lindsay Konjoian

SERVES: 6 | PREP TIME: 10 MINUTES | COOK TIME: 30 MINUTES

INGREDIENTS

12 ounces pasta, such as rigatoni or ziti
2 tablespoons extra-virgin olive oil
1 large onion, diced
1 ½ teaspoons salt
4 cloves garlic, finely chopped
1 bell pepper, diced
8 ounces mushrooms, sliced
2 teaspoons dry Italian seasoning
¼ teaspoon ground pepper
5 ounces baby spinach
1 14-ounce can crushed tomatoes, preferably fire-roasted tomatoes
½ cup fresh basil, chopped
8 ounces (1 cup) part-skim ricotta cheese or plant-based ricotta
2 cups shredded cheese, such as cheddar, an Italian cheese blend, or Italian-style vegan cheese shreds

INSTRUCTIONS

1. Bring a large pot of lightly salted water to a boil. Add the pasta, and cook it according to the package instructions for al dente pasta. Meanwhile, preheat the oven to 400°F, and coat a 9" × 13" casserole dish with cooking spray.
2. After the pasta is ready, drain it well in a colander, and run cool water over it to wash off extra starch and to prevent the pasta from clumping together. Return the pasta to the pot.

3. Heat the olive oil in a large skillet over medium-high heat. Add the onion and salt. Cook the onion, stirring often, until the onion has softened and is starting to brown, 6–7 minutes. Add the garlic, bell pepper, mushrooms, Italian seasoning, and pepper. Cook the vegetables, stirring often, until they are tender and any excess moisture has evaporated, 7–8 minutes. Stir in the spinach, and continue cooking until the spinach has just wilted, about 1 minute.
4. Add the vegetable mixture, crushed tomatoes, and basil to the pasta, and stir everything together well. (Sausage could be added at this stage for a flexitarian option.)
5. Transfer the pasta and veggie mixture to the casserole dish. Dollop the ricotta over the top of the pasta, and top the casserole with the shredded cheese.
6. Bake the pasta until it is bubbling hot and the cheese has melted, about 12 minutes. Let it cool at least 5 minutes before serving.

CHICKEN JAMBALAYA RECIPE

by James Overbeck

SERVES: 10 FIREMEN | PREP TIME: 30 MINUTES | COOK TIME 1 HOUR

INGREDIENTS:

7 chicken breasts (boil)
3 smoked sausage
2 yellow onions (chopped)
6 sticks celery (chopped)
2 green peppers (chopped)
4 x 16oz cans black eyed peas
2 large cans diced tomatoes
4 cans water
1 ½ teaspoon cayenne red pepper
1 teaspoon white pepper
2 tablespoons black pepper
6 tablespoons Cajun seasoning
1 tablespoon minced garlic
½ tablespoon horseradish
1 tablespoon Tony Chachere's
Gumbo File
Rice
Crackers

INSTRUCTIONS

1. Bring a large pan of water to boil
2. Clean up the chicken breasts and boil them for about 15 minutes or until thoroughly cooked, once cool enough, dice up the chicken.
3. Cut up smoked sausage
4. Sauté chopped onion, celery & peppers in a skillet
5. Add all other ingredients in to a big pot
6. Add Cajun, cayenne and gumbo file seasoning slowly and season to taste
7. Bring to boil and then let simmer for at least an hour.

I was given this recipe by one of my friends who is a firemen. Of course the quantities in the recipe reflect those of a firehouse kitchen. Unless you have a firehouse size family, you're going to need to adjust the quantities. Get yourself a big beer or a glass of wine and enjoy—a food coma is sure to follow!

SIDES

AVOCADO AND TOMATO SALAD

By Pauline Lacroix

SERVES: 4 | PREP TIME: 15 MINUTES

INGREDIENTS

1 ½ pints mixed-colored cherry tomatoes, sliced into halves
¼ cup purple onions, sliced into bite-size pieces
½ ripe avocado, sliced into bite-size pieces
2 tablespoons light olive oil
¼ cup red wine vinegar
Salt, to taste

INSTRUCTIONS

1. Mix the first 3 ingredients together, and then add in the olive oil and red wine vinegar.
2. Sprinkle the salad with salt before serving.

BACON AND BROCCOLI SALAD

By Olivia Grohe

SERVES: 4–6 | PREP TIME: 30 MINUTES | REFRIGERATOR TIME: 3–4 HOURS (FOR OPTIMAL TASTE)

INGREDIENTS

3 heads broccoli (or 2 bags precut broccoli)
12 strips bacon
2 cups sharp cheddar cheese, grated
1 small onion, diced

The Dressing
1 cup mayonnaise
¼ cup sugar
3 tablespoons vinegar

INSTRUCTIONS

1. Wash the broccoli, and cut it into bite-size pieces (if not already cut).
2. Cook the bacon until crispy and, once cool to the touch, crumble it.
3. Mix the broccoli, grated cheese, diced onion, and bacon in a large mixing bowl.
4. Mix the dressing ingredients separately, pour the mixture into the mixing bowl over the other ingredients, and stir the salad to coat the ingredients evenly.
5. Refrigerate the salad for 3–4 hours prior to serving for optimal taste.

CROCK-POT MAC AND CHEESE

By Rachelle Goldhammer

SERVES: 8–10 | PREP TIME: 10 MINUTES | COOK TIME: 4 HOURS

INGREDIENTS

1 pound elbow macaroni
½ cup butter, melted
1 12-ounce can evaporated milk
1 12-ounce can cheddar cheese soup
1 cup milk
4 cups shredded cheddar cheese
2 eggs, beaten

INSTRUCTIONS

1. Boil the macaroni, then drain it and put it in a Crock-Pot. (An oval Crock-Pot works best!)
2. Pour the melted butter over the macaroni.
3. In a small bowl, mix all the other ingredients together, pour the mixture over the macaroni, and stir to combine.
4. Cook on low for 4 hours.

GERMAN POTATO SALAD

By Michael Farmer

SERVES: 4–6 | PREP TIME: 10 MINUTES | COOK TIME: 50 MINUTES

INGREDIENTS

1–2 pounds bacon (to taste)
5 pounds red potatoes
1 16-ounce jar Wickles pickles, diced (or 1 cup diced celery, if preferred)
¾ cup white vinegar
¼ cup water
1 cup sugar
1 tablespoon flour
1 large yellow onion, diced
Salt and pepper, to taste

INSTRUCTIONS

1. Fry the bacon, remove it from the frying pan, and dice it. Leave the majority of the bacon grease in the frying pan for later use.
2. While the bacon is cooking, place the potatoes in a large pot, cover them with water, and boil them until tender. Once the potatoes are tender, drain the water, and cut the potatoes into chunks, leaving them in the pot.
3. Layer the diced bacon and pickles over the potatoes.
4. In a large measuring cup, mix the vinegar, water, sugar and flour, then pour the mixture into the frying pan.
5. Bring the mix to a boil, then add the onion. Turn down the heat, and let the mixture simmer for a couple of minutes, just long enough to soften the onion.
6. Remove the mixture from the frying pan, pour it over the potatoes/bacon/pickles in the pot, and stir gently to combine.
7. Add salt and pepper to taste.

GRANDMA'S HOMEMADE ROLLS

By Amanda Anderson

YIELD: 18 ROLLS | PREP TIME: 4½ HOURS | COOK TIME: 20 MINUTES

INGREDIENTS

2 cups milk
½ cup sugar
1 tablespoon salt

2 eggs, beaten
6 tablespoons vegetable oil
1 cup flour

2 packages yeast
½ cup hot water

6–8 cups flour

INSTRUCTIONS

1. Bring the milk to a boil. Watch it carefully so it does not boil over.
2. Stir in the sugar and salt, let the milk cool.
3. Once the milk has cooled (after about 20 minutes), stir in the beaten eggs, oil, and flour.
4. Dissolve the yeast in the hot water, and add it to the milk mixture.
5. Then alternate adding 1 cup of flour at a time with mixing/kneading, until all the flour (about 6–8 cups) has been added. The dough should be smooth and slightly tacky to the touch. If it's too sticky, add more flour ¼ cup at a time.
6. I was taught to knead by hand. But, since it is modern times, I do use my KitchenAid mixer with the dough kneading hook. Knead by hand for 8 minutes or 4 minutes on medium speed if using a mixer.
7. Cover the dough with a light towel, and let it rise for 4 hours. I put the dough in my microwave (somewhere with no draft).

8. After 4 hours, punch the dough down, and make it into rolls. Divide dough into 18 portions. Then roll the dough into a ball shape and put on the baking sheet(s). Let them continue to rise on a baking sheet for 20–30 minutes.
9. Preheat the oven to 350°F. Bake the rolls for 20 minutes.

GREEK LEMON RICE

By Pauline Lacroix

SERVES: 4 | PREP TIME: 10 MINUTES | COOK TIME: 22 MINUTES

INGREDIENTS

2 tablespoons butter
½ cup diced purple onion
1 cup long-grain rice
2 tablespoons orzo
2 cups chicken stock
3 ounces lemon juice (divided)
2 tablespoons chopped parsley

INSTRUCTIONS

1. In a small saucepan, heat the butter, and add the onion, cooking it until soft. Then add the rice and orzo, and continue cooking for about 4 minutes, stirring frequently.
2. Add the chicken stock and 2 ounces of the lemon juice, and bring the stock to a light boil. Then reduce the heat to low, cover, and cook for 20 minutes or until the liquid has been absorbed by the rice.
3. Remove the rice from the heat, and gently fold in the remaining 1 ounce of lemon juice and the parsley.

The rice goes great with chicken souvlaki (page 48) and Greek salad (page 115)!

GREEK SALAD

By Pauline Lacroix

SERVES: 4 | PREP TIME: 15 MINUTES

INGREDIENTS

The Salad Dressing

2 garlic cloves, minced
1 teaspoon dried oregano
½ teaspoon Dijon mustard
¼ cup red wine vinegar
1 teaspoon salt
½ teaspoon freshly ground pepper
½ cup olive oil

The Salad

1 English cucumber, sliced (¼" thick)
4 ounces feta cheese, diced
1 red pepper, diced in large pieces
½ cup Kalamata olives, pitted and sliced
½ purple/red onion, diced in large pieces
1 ½ pints multicolored cherry tomatoes, sliced into halves

INSTRUCTIONS

1. Combine the garlic, oregano, mustard, red wine vinegar, salt, and pepper in a small bowl.
2. While constantly whisking, slowly add the olive oil so that it emulsifies.
3. Add the dressing to salad ingredients 10 minutes prior to serving, and add a bit of salt to perk up the flavors.

The salad goes great with chicken souvlaki (page 48) and Greek lemon rice (page 114)

HAPPY POTATO SALAD

By Traci Anderson

SERVES: 6–8 | PREP TIME: 30 MINUTES | COOK TIME: 60 MINUTES

INGREDIENTS

¾ pound white potatoes (8 medium potatoes), peeled and cut into 1" quarters
¾ pound sweet potatoes (8 medium potatoes), peeled and cut into 1" quarters

The Dressing

1 ½ cups mayonnaise (or ¾ cup garlic- and rosemary-infused olive oil)
½ cup sour cream (or, if using olive oil, ¼ cup of any vinegar)
1 teaspoon onion powder
1 teaspoon garlic powder
½ teaspoon celery seed (or mustard seed)

¼ cup celery, diced
¼ cup sweet onion, diced
Salt and pepper, to taste

Optional Toppings

4 green onions, chopped
Fresh parsley, chopped
¼ teaspoon paprika

INSTRUCTIONS

The Potatoes

1. Bring a pot of water to a boil.
2. Add the white potatoes, and cook them for 3 minutes.
3. To the same water, add the sweet potatoes, and cook them for 10 minutes or until all the potatoes are tender.
4. Drain the potatoes, and place them in a large mixing bowl. Refrigerate them for 30 minutes.

The Dressing

1. Mix the mayo and sour cream (or oil and vinegar); stir in the onion powder, garlic powder, and celery seed (or mustard seed).

To Combine

1. Add the diced celery and onion to the potatoes in the large mixing bowl, and lightly toss the ingredients together.
2. To evenly mix in the dressing, add ½ the dressing to the potatoes, and lightly toss. Then, repeat with remaining dressing.
3. Add salt and pepper to taste.
4. Garnish with the green onions, parsley, and/or paprika.
5. Refrigerate the salad for 1 hour or more before serving.

HARICOTS VERTS PROVENCE

By Pauline Lacroix

SERVES: 4 | PREP TIME: 20 MINUTES | COOK TIME: 2 MINUTES

INGREDIENTS

2 tablespoons olive oil
2 tablespoons shallots, finely diced
2 garlic cloves, pureed with a garlic press of the side of a knife
1 pound French green beans (haricots verts), trimmed
1 tablespoon fresh tarragon, chopped
1 teaspoon lemon zest
2 tablespoons pine nuts, toasted
Salt and pepper, to taste

INSTRUCTIONS

1. Heat a large sauté pan (or wok) over medium heat, and add the olive oil. Sauté the shallots until they are translucent, then add the garlic. Sauté 1 minute more, then set the shallots and garlic aside and cover them keep them warm.
2. Bring a large pot of salted water to a rolling boil, then add the green beans, and cook for 2 minutes or until they snap and are tender. Remove the beans from the water, drain them well, then immediately add them to the shallot-garlic oil (the *sauce Provençale).*
3. Add the herbs and lemon zest, and season with salt and pepper to taste.
4. Sprinkle the beans with the pine nuts, then serve immediately.

ROASTED ROOT VEGETABLES

By Pauline Lacroix

SERVES: 4 | PREP TIME: 10 MINUTES | COOK TIME: 30 MINUTES

INGREDIENTS

¼ cup butter

2 tablespoons olive oil

4 carrots, peeled and sliced a ½" thick on the bias

½ celery root, peeled and sliced on the bias (same size as the carrots)

4 parsnips, peeled and sliced on the bias (same size as the carrots)

2 tablespoons dried thyme

2 tablespoons dried parsley

2 cloves garlic, pureed with a garlic press of the side of a knife

1 teaspoon cayenne pepper

Salt and pepper, to taste

INSTRUCTIONS

1. Preheat the oven to 375°F.
2. Preheat a frying pan (that can go into the oven) over high heat. Add the butter, olive oil, and root vegetables, and sear the vegetables to an even color.
3. Season the vegetables with the herbs, garlic, cayenne, salt, and pepper.
4. Finish cooking the vegetables in the oven for 20–25 minutes, or until fork tender.

SCALLOPED POTATOES

By Pauline Lacroix

SERVES: 6 | PREP TIME: 25 MINUTES | COOK TIME: 90 MINUTES

INGREDIENTS

1 10.5-ounce can condensed cream of mushroom soup
1 can milk (measured with the empty soup can)
6–8 medium Yukon Gold potatoes, thinly and evenly sliced so they cook evenly
½ cup green bell pepper, chopped
½ cup green onions, chopped
2 tablespoons flour
Salt and pepper, to taste
4 ounces cheddar or Gruyere cheese, grated (about 1 cup)

INSTRUCTIONS

1. Preheat the oven to 350°F.
2. In a small bowl, mix the soup and milk together.
3. Spray a 9" × 13" baking dish.
4. Place a layer of potatoes on the bottom of the dish. Sprinkle a mixture of green peppers and green onions over the potatoes, then some flour and salt and pepper. Repeat this for 3 more layers.
5. On the 4th layer of potatoes, pour the soup and milk mixture, and top this layer with the cheese. (Note: the sauce will bubble over the dish in the oven.)

6. Cover the baking dish with aluminum foil, and bake the potatoes for 75 minutes. Then remove the aluminum foil, and bake for another 15 minutes.
7. The scalloped potatoes are cooked when a knife or fork goes through them easily.

Tips

- Put a baking sheet under the baking dish to catch any bubbled-over sauce.
- The potatoes are even better when served the next day.

SUNSHINE BROCCOLI SALAD

By Janette Gawlikowski

SERVES: 4 | PREP TIME: 15–20 MINUTES

INGREDIENTS

The Dressing

½ teaspoon minced garlic (one clove)
½ teaspoon turmeric
2 tablespoons extra-virgin olive oil
1 tablespoon apple cider vinegar
2 tablespoons mayo (good quality, vegan is OK)
2–3 tablespoons raw honey
Juice and zest of 1 lemon

The Salad

2 cups chopped broccoli (approximately 1 head)
1 red bell pepper, chopped
1 crispy apple, diced but unpeeled
¼ cup sunflower seeds (any type)
¼ cup raisins (brown or golden) or ¼ cup dried cherries, chopped

INSTRUCTIONS

1. Combine all dressing ingredients in a bowl, and whisk them together well.
2. Put all salad ingredients in a bowl, and stir.
3. Add the dressing to the salad, and mix it together well. Enjoy!

Tips

- For more crunch (and if you really like to chop veggies), add 1–2 stalks of diced celery and/or 1–2 diced carrots.
- Add any type of nut you prefer, chopped.
- Store the salad in the refrigerator, tightly covered, for up to 2 days.

TORTILLA SOUP

By Maritza Escalante

SERVES: 4 | PREP TIME: 15 MINUTES | COOK TIME: 15–20 MINUTES

INGREDIENTS

4 corn tortillas, a few days old
1 tablespoon vegetable oil, plus extra for frying
1 small onion, finely chopped
2 garlic cloves, crushed
2 large carrots, peeled and diced
4 cups low-sodium chicken stock or vegetable stock
½ cup frozen or canned green peas (or chopped green beans or celery)
Knorr granulated Tomato Bouillon with Chicken Flavor, to taste
Ground white pepper, to taste

Optional

1 cup rotisserie chicken, shredded (usually left over from a previous meal)
1 small bunch cilantro, washed, dried, and chopped
1 lemon, quartered
1 avocado, sliced

INSTRUCTIONS

1. Using a sharp knife, cut each tortilla into 4 or 5 strips, each measuring about ¾" wide.
2. Pour vegetable oil into a heavy frying pan to a depth of ¾". Heat the oil until a small piece of tortilla added to the oil floats to the top and bubbles around the edges.
3. Add a few tortilla strips to the hot oil. Fry them for a few minutes, until crisp and golden brown all over, turning them occasionally. Remove the tortilla strips with a slotted spoon, and drain them on a double layer of paper towels. Cook the remaining tortilla strips the same way.

(cont'd)

4. Heat 1 tablespoon vegetable oil in a large, heavy saucepan. Add the chopped onion and garlic, and cook them over medium heat for 2–3 minutes, stirring constantly with a wooden spatula, until the onion is soft and translucent. Do not let the garlic turn brown, or it will give the soup a bitter taste.
5. Add the carrots to the onion mixture, white pepper and chicken bouillon in the pan. Pour in the chicken stock (or vegetable stock), and stir well. Bring it to a boil, then lower the heat.
6. Add the peas (or green beans) and the rotisserie chicken and let the soup simmer for about 5 minutes, until the liquid has reduced slightly.
7. Place a few strips of the crisp tortilla pieces in the bottom of four warmed soup bowls. Ladle the soup on top of the tortilla pieces. Sprinkle each bowl with the chopped cilantro. Squeeze a quarter of lemon for a tangy, refreshing flavor. Add the sliced avocado. *Buen apetito!*

WATERMELON, FETA, AND ARUGULA SALAD

By Bonnie Sparkman

SERVES: 4–6 | PREP TIME: 15 MINUTES

INGREDIENTS

The Vinaigrette

¼ cup freshly squeezed orange juice
¼ cup freshly squeezed lemon juice (from 2 lemons)
1 large shallot, minced (¼ cup)
1 tablespoon honey
1 teaspoon kosher salt
½ teaspoon freshly ground black pepper
½ cup good olive oil

The Salad

5 ounces baby arugula, washed and spun dry
4 cups seedless watermelon, rind removed, cut in bite-size cubes
6–12 ounces crumbled feta cheese (or ½" cubes)
4 ounces fresh mint leaves, julienned
Optional: For the Fourth of July, add blueberries to make the salad red, white, and blue.

(cont'd)

INSTRUCTIONS

1. Whisk together the orange juice, lemon juice, shallot, honey, salt, and pepper. Slowly pour in the olive oil, whisking constantly to form an emulsion. If the vinaigrette is not used within an hour, store it, covered, in the refrigerator.
2. Place the arugula, watermelon, feta, and mint (and blueberries, if using) in a large bowl. Drizzle the salad with enough vinaigrette to coat the greens lightly, and toss it well. Taste and adjust for seasonings, then serve the salad immediately.

Tip: Be careful to dress the salad just before serving. The vinaigrette will break down the salad quickly, and it's not something you can save.

DRINKS

A PROPER CUP OF ENGLISH TEA

By Darius Goodall

SERVES: 1 | PREP TIME: AS QUICKLY AS YOU CAN

INGREDIENTS

Some amount of your favorite whiskey or single malt
1 fat Hoyo/Cuban
1 fireplace
1 suitably tied robe

INSTRUCTIONS

Really? I mean, add an ice cube if you must! And...don't forget to raise that pinky—it is, after all, A Proper Cup of English Tea"!

BLACKBERRY SUMMER MOCKTAIL

By Sheryl Howley Johnson

SERVES: 2 | PREP TIME: 15 MINUTES

INGREDIENTS

Mocktail

1 cup blackberries
¼ cup honey
1 sprig mint
1 lemon, juiced
½ cup water
2 cups seltzer water

Garnish

5 blackberries
2 mint leaves

INSTRUCTIONS

1. To a cocktail shaker, add the blackberries, honey, and mint, then muddle them until well blended. (Muddling pushes together the ingredients and mushes the berries and damages the herbs, which allows the flavors to impart better with the liquids.)
2. Then, to the cocktail shaker, add the lemon juice and water. Put the lid on, then shake to mix well.
3. Pour the mixture evenly into two normal glasses or four small glasses.
4. Top each glass with seltzer water.
5. Garnish each glass with the blackberries and mint.

DZ'S "PINEAPPLE PUNCH IN THE FACE" COCKTAIL

By Dave Zaro

SERVES: 10 | PREP TIME: 30 MINUTES | INFUSION TIME: 12 DAYS

This remarkable concoction was delivered to me from a very famous bartender on Fifth Avenue in New York in 2007. I sat with this inventor for weeks to learn the technique of pineapple choosing, the cutting of the fruit, the correct amount of vodka. Nothing short of perfection was achieved.

Please take your time to perfect this cocktail. It makes a wonderful pre-dinner martini, before you head to your local bistro. Don't drive after one of these—or operate farm machinery or handle beehive maintenance.

INGREDIENTS

1 fresh whole pineapple
1 750 ml Tito's vodka
1 wide-mouthed, glass, gallon-sized (or bigger) jug, with a tight top
Frozen pineapple chunks (for garnish)

INSTRUCTIONS

Infusing the Vodka

1. Trim the sides of the pineapple.
2. Cut the pineapple into rings about ¾" wide.
3. Lay each ring inside the glass jug, and stack them on each other.
4. Pour the entire bottle of vodka in the jug, and seal the top.
5. Place the jug in a cool, dry place, out of the sun, for 14*days*.
6. The pineapple rings will become lighter in color as the juice is extracted into the vodka, and they will begin to sink below the vodka line.

(cont'd)

7. On the 14th day, you can either do the following step with a juicer machine—like I use (the best)—or use your hands. Remove the pineapple slices from the vodka, and place them in the juicer until they have all been juiced. Take the juice, and pour it back into the jug with the vodka. If using your hands to squeeze the fruit, do it over or inside the jug.
8. Throw out fruit when done.
9. Through a strainer, pour the vodka juice from the jug into a 16-ounce (or bigger) glass bottle. (The Container Store sells them with a closed top.)
10. With a whole jug, I can fill up at least two bottles.

To Serve

1. Chill a martini glass in the freezer.
2. Add ice to a martini shaker, and pour in the juice mixture.
3. Shake as if your life depended on it.
4. Pour the cocktail into the chilled martini glass (or serve the drink on the rocks). Garnish with a frozen pineapple chunk, placed into the drink.

FRENCH 75

By Christie Brusilow

SERVES: 1 | PREP TIME: 7 MINUTES

INGREDIENTS

1 ounce gin
½ ounce lemon juice
½ teaspoon simple syrup or superfine sugar
2 ounces champagne or prosecco
1 lemon peel

Notes

- Use Meyer lemon if it is in season.
- You can skip the simple syrup if you are using a sweeter prosecco.

INSTRUCTIONS

1. In a shaker filled with ice, add the gin, lemon juice, and simple syrup.
2. Shake the cocktail well, and strain it into a champagne flute.
3. Top the cocktail with the champagne or prosecco.
4. Garnish with the lemon peel.

HOMEMADE BAILEYS

By Sheri Stuckey

SERVES: 4 | PREP TIME: 10 MINUTES

INGREDIENTS

1 cup heavy cream

1 14-ounce can sweetened condensed milk

3 tablespoons chocolate syrup

1 teaspoon instant coffee granules

1 teaspoon vanilla extract

1 ⅔ cups Jameson Triple Distilled Irish Whiskey

INSTRUCTIONS

1. In a blender, place the cream, sweetened condensed milk, chocolate syrup, instant coffee granules, and vanilla extract. Blend on low speed for 30–60 seconds.
2. Slowly add half of the Jameson whiskey, and mix well on low speed for 30–60 seconds. Then add the other half of the whiskey, blending on low for another 30–60 seconds. Adding the whiskey slowly ensures that it will incorporate evenly and not separate.
3. To enjoy, pour the "Baileys" over ice as a cocktail, or add it to your coffee or over ice cream.

Tips

- Store the Baileys in the refrigerator in a sterile glass bottle with a tight lid.
- Shake it well before enjoying.
- Store it up to one month.

HOT SPICED BOURBON COCKTAIL

By Pauline Lacroix

SERVES: 4 | PREP TIME: 20 MINUTES | COOK TIME: 90 MINUTES

INGREDIENTS

4 bags Earl Grey tea
20 ounces hot water
4 cinnamon sticks
4 star anise
4 ounces bourbon
8 teaspoons honey
Juice from ½ a lemon
4 orange slices

INSTRUCTIONS

1. Place the tea bags into the hot water with the cinnamon sticks and star anise, and let the tea steep for about 3 minutes.
2. Take the tea bags out of the hot water, and mix in the bourbon, honey, and lemon juice.
3. Pour the cocktail mixture into a mug or toddy glass, and garnish it with a cinnamon stick, star anise, and orange slice.

PALOMA

By Laura Kelly

SERVES: 1 | PREP TIME: 5 MINUTES

INGREDIENTS

½ ounce fresh-squeezed lime juice
1 ½ ounces tequila
2 ounces grapefruit juice
4 ounces grapefruit beer
Splenda (optional)

INSTRUCTIONS

1. Fill your favorite glass with ice.
2. Add all the ingredients.
3. Add more grapefruit juice or Splenda if you'd like your drink a little sweeter.

ROSEMARY WHISKEY SOUR

By Courtney Radke

SERVES: 2 | PREP TIME: 5–10 MINUTES | COOK TIME: 10 MINUTES

INGREDIENTS

3 ounces bourbon
2 ounces fresh lemon juice
1 ounce simple syrup
1–2 egg whites, either 1 large egg white or
2 medium (optional)
Rosemary sprig
Ice cubes (for shaking)

Garnishes
Lemon slices
Rosemary sprigs
Brandied cherries

INSTRUCTIONS

1. Add all the wet ingredients and 1 rosemary sprig into a cocktail shaker, without ice, and shake vigorously for 10–15 seconds. This initial dry shake helps ensure proper mixture and foaming of the egg whites. (Be careful when removing the lid as foam might have accumulated at the top.)
2. Next, add ice cubes (5–6 should do), and give a moderate shake for another 10–15 seconds.
3. Grab your nicest rocks glass, and strain your beautiful, bourbony-lemony drink evenly. The drink should be cloudy and have a nice foamy head if you opted for the egg whites.
4. Add a few lemon slices to the top (or rim) of your drinks along with a sprig of rosemary and a brandied cherry (or 2) per glass to complete the presentation. Enjoy!

(cont'd)

Notes

- If your drink isn't foamy, then you didn't shake hard enough or long enough on the dry shake. Don't worry. It will still taste fine, but be sure to shake vigorously next time. Also be sure to use fresh eggs!
- *I opt for making homemade simple syrup and add rosemary as it heats up to impart flavor. It's simple to make with a one-to-one ratio of granulated sugar to water, heated slowly on the stove until the sugar dissolves (about 10 minutes). You can bottle up what you don't use and save it for later—or immediately after, for your next drink! Get creative, and add other ingredients to the syrup to suit your taste or drink of choice.

VIRGIN TONIC AND BITTERS

By Darius Goodall

SERVES: 1 | PREP TIME: 2 MINUTES

This makes for a great, refreshing summer cocktail. You could, of course, add a splash of your favorite poison. But, as it comes, it's full of fragrant flavors and aromas to tantalize the most discerning taste buds!

INGREDIENTS

Ice
1 squeeze of lime juice
1–3 splashes Angostura bitters
tonic
Mint or rosemary to garnish

INSTRUCTIONS

1. Fill a glass of your choosing with ice.
2. Mix in the lime juice, bitters, and tonic (enough to fill the glass).
3. Garnish and enjoy!

DESSERTS

APPLE TARTE TATIN WITH CRÈME ANGLAISE

By Pauline Lacroix

SERVES: 6 | PREP TIME: 15 MINUTES | COOK TIME: 30 MINUTES

INGREDIENTS

Tarte Tatin

½ cup granulated sugar

3 tablespoons cold water

2 tablespoons butter

3 Granny Smith apples, peeled, cored, and each cut into 6 pieces

1 puff pastry sheet, thawed

Crème Anglaise

1 cup (250 ml) 35 percent cream (whipping cream)

2 ounces granulated sugar

½ tablespoon vanilla

3 eggs yolks, whisked

Vanilla ice cream (optional side)

INSTRUCTIONS

Tarte Tatin

1. Preheat the oven to 375°F.
2. In an 8" frying pan (that can go into the oven), add the sugar and water, and heat the syrup on a medium heat until a golden-brown color is achieved. Do not mix the syrup; just swirl it occasionally. If the caramel gets smoky, remove it from the heat for 30 seconds, then put it back on the stove. Once the caramel is golden, take it off the heat. Then add the butter, and swirl to combine.
3. Lay the apples in the pan—starting around the outside of pan and working toward the middle.

(cont'd)

4. Place the puff pastry on top of the apples, and fold over the edges.
5. Bake the tart in the oven for about 18 minutes or until the pastry is golden and crisp.
6. Remove the tart from the oven, and invert it onto a large serving plate. Serve it with vanilla ice cream and/or crème anglaise.

Crème Anglaise

1. In a small saucepan, add the cream, sugar, and vanilla, and heat the mixture just to a boil. Remove the cream from the heat.
2. While whisking, slowly pour the hot cream mixture over the whisked egg yolks until all the cream has been incorporated.
3. Return the cream to the saucepan and, over low to medium heat, slowly bring the cream to an "almost boil (just starts to show small bubbles)." (Do not boil for very long—or this mixture will turn into scrambled egg.) The mixture will thicken slightly, then remove it from heat, strain it, and set it aside. Let it cool, then serve it with dessert.

CHILLED STRAWBERRY CHEESECAKE

By Laura Kelly

SERVES: 8 | PREP TIME: 45 MINUTES | COOK/CHILL TIME: 4 HOURS

INGREDIENTS

The Crust

1 stick butter, melted

2 cups graham cracker crumbs

6 tablespoons powdered sugar

Cooking spray

The Filling

1 8-ounce pack cream cheese

1 ½ cups powdered sugar (divided)

1 ½ teaspoons vanilla (divided)

1 pack Dream Whip

½ cup milk

The Strawberry Topping

16 ounces frozen sliced strawberries

2 tablespoons cornstarch

½ cup sugar

INSTRUCTIONS

The Crust

1. In a small bowl, mix together well the melted butter, crushed graham crackers, and powdered sugar.
2. Spray a glass 9" pie pan with cooking spray, and press the crust mixture into the pan. Put the crust into the refrigerator to cool and harden.

(cont'd)

The Filling

1. With a mixer, mix together the cream cheese, 1 cup of the powdered sugar, and 1 teaspoon of the vanilla. Set the cream cheese mixture aside.
2. Prepare the Dream Whip as instructed on the package, with the milk and remaining ½ teaspoon vanilla. This is important: use a mixer for a full 5 minutes to whip it. Add the remaining ½ cup powdered sugar to the mixture.

Assembly

1. Gently fold together the two fillings to make one. Spread this mixture into the cooled crust, and put it back in the refrigerator.
2. In a saucepan over high heat, cook the strawberries, cornstarch, and sugar. Stir while heating the mixture to a boil, then let it boil for about a minute. Pull it off the heat, and set it aside to cool.
3. Once the topping has cooled completely, spread it on top of the pie, and put the pie back into the refrigerator to cool for a couple more hours before serving. Leftovers should be stored in the refrigerator.

HOMEMADE CHIPWICH

By Sheryl Howley Johnson

SERVES: 10 | PREP TIME: 30 MINUTES | COOK TIME: 12 MINUTES

INGREDIENTS

The Cookies

1 ¼ cups unbleached all-purpose flour
½ teaspoon baking soda
½ teaspoon salt
7 tablespoons unsalted butter, room temperature
¾ cups brown sugar, packed
2 tablespoons granulated sugar
1 large egg, room temperature
1 teaspoon vanilla
1 cup mini chocolate chips

The Ice Cream Sandwich

½ gallon vanilla ice cream
1 cup mini chocolate chips

INSTRUCTIONS

The Cookies

1. Preheat the oven to 350°F. Line a baking sheet with parchment paper, and set it aside.
2. In a medium bowl, whisk together the flour, baking soda, and salt. Set it aside.
3. In the bowl of a stand mixer fitted with a paddle attachment, beat on medium speed the butter, brown sugar, and granulated sugar until light and fluffy, about 4 minutes. Scrape down the sides of the bowl when necessary. Add the egg and vanilla. Beat until combined, 20–30 seconds.

(cont'd)

4. With the mixer on low, slowly add the flour mixture to the dough, being careful not to overbeat. With a wooden spoon or rubber spatula, stir in the chocolate chips by hand.
5. Scoop about 2 tablespoons of the cookie dough, shape it into a ball, and place it onto the prepared baking sheet. Press down on the dough slightly, with your hand or the back of a measuring cup. Repeat, placing each ball of cookie dough about 1" to 2" apart. Bake the cookies for about 12 minutes or until the edges start to turn brown. Remove the cookies from the oven, cool them on the pan for 5 minutes, and then transfer them to a wire rack to cool completely. Transfer the cookies to the freezer for 20–30 minutes.

The Ice Cream Sandwich Assembly

1. Take one cookie, and place a scoop of ice cream (about ¼ cup) on the flat side of the cookie. Top the ice cream with the flat side of a second cookie to make a sandwich.
2. Place mini chocolate chips in a bowl or on a plate. Roll the sides of the sandwich in the chips. Serve the ice cream sandwiches immediately, or wrap them tightly in plastic wrap and freeze them.

Notes

- Transferring the chocolate chip cookies to the freezer is essential. If you try to make the sandwiches with warm or room temperature cookies, the cookies will break when you press the ice cream between them. You will also get chocolate chips all over your hands!
- Storing homemade chipwiches: Once you have assembled the ice cream sandwiches, let them harden in the freezer for an hour. Then, individually wrap them in plastic wrap, or place them in reusable storage bags. Chipwiches will keep in the freezer for up to a month.

CHOCOLATE DEPRESSION CAKE

By Bonnie Sparkman

SERVES: 9 | PREP TIME: 10 MINUTES | COOK TIME: 35 MINUTES

INGREDIENTS

The Cake

1 ½ cups all-purpose flour (180 grams)
¼ cup unsweetened cocoa powder
1 cup sugar
½ teaspoon salt
1 teaspoon baking soda
1 tablespoon white vinegar
1 teaspoon vanilla extract
5 tablespoons vegetable oil
1 cup lukewarm water

OPTIONAL FROSTINGS

Chocolate Ganache

1 cup heavy cream
8.75 ounces bittersweet or dark chocolate, chopped (or use chips)
1 stick unsalted butter

Vanilla-Strawberry Buttercream

Vanilla buttercream (prepared)
1.2 ounces freeze-dried strawberries

INSTRUCTIONS

The Cake

1. Add the flour, cocoa powder, sugar, salt, and baking soda directly to a cake pan—with dimensions 8" × 8" × 2". Mix everything with a wooden spoon.
2. Make depressions in the dry ingredients: add the vinegar in a tablespoon-sized depression; add the vanilla extract in a teaspoon-sized depression; and add the oil in 5 tablespoon-sized depressions.
3. Pour the water over everything, and mix everything with a wooden spoon until you have a smooth batter.
4. Bake the cake at 350°F for 35 minutes or until an inserted toothpick comes out clean.
5. Let the cake cool to room temperature.

(cont'd)

Notes

- Yes, you can mix everything in the pan and save on doing dishes! However, the cake will stick to the pan slightly since the pan can't be lined or sprayed. Just leave the cake in the pan, and use a plastic knife and offset spatula to serve. If you want a prettier presentation, use a mixing bowl and a greased/lined 8" round pan.
- You can make this cake gluten-free if you substitute King Arthur Measure for Measure gluten-free flour for the all-purpose flour. (The picture above is a cake made with gluten-free flour!)
- If you use either frosting option, this cake is no longer vegan.

Chocolate Ganache

1. Warm the heavy cream in a heavy, stainless steel pot until warm.
2. Add the chocolate and the butter.
3. Stir the chocolate over low heat until it has almost melted.
4. Take the pot off the heat, and stir the ganache until smooth.
5. Let it cool slightly. Then, when it has slightly thickened, whisk it and pour it over the cake. Smooth it with a spatula.
6. For a perfect glossy finish, refrigerate the cake with one coat of the ganache on top. When the first coat is cold and set, add another portion of the ganache, and smooth it nicely with a spatula. (If the pot of ganache has hardened while you waited, reheat it for just a few seconds to the desired consistency, and whisk it again before pouring the second coat.) If you prefer a more frosting-like look, instead of a shiny/glossy look, whisk the ganache without warming it up, and spread it with an offset spatula.

Tip: Should there be any leftovers, the ganache, as a kind of fondue, is great for dipping fresh or dried fruit.

Strawberry-Vanilla Buttercream

1. Start with your favorite vanilla buttercream recipe, or I also highly recommend King Arthur buttercream in a box.
2. In a food processor, pulverize the freeze-dried strawberries into a fine powder. (I use Trader Joe's freeze-dried strawberries.)
3. When adding the dry ingredients for your vanilla buttercream recipe, mix in the strawberry powder. Add a touch more liquid if you find the buttercream too dry—if, for example, you decided you needed to add in more strawberry powder. (For boxed buttercream, simply fold in the strawberry powder.)
4. Give the strawberry flavor time to fully permeate the buttercream, so prepare the buttercream a few hours in advance of serving.

Tip: You can also add the strawberry powder to a cream cheese frosting,

GAVIN'S CHOCOLATE OOZE CAKE

By Regina Gruezo

SERVES: 8 | PREP TIME: 25 MINUTES | COOK TIME: 12 MINUTES

INGREDIENTS

Chocolate Ganache

1 cup dark chocolate chips
½ cup heavy cream

Cake Mixture

1 ½ cups dark chocolate chips
½ cup plus 2 tablespoons butter

4 whole eggs
4 egg yolks
⅔ cup light brown sugar
1 teaspoon salt
2 teaspoons vanilla extract
¼ cup all-purpose flour

Prepping the Ramekins

¼ cup butter, softened
½ cup sugar

½ cup powdered sugar (for finishing)
Berries, ice cream, and/or rock salt (optional garnishes/sides)

INSTRUCTIONS

Prep the ganache 20–30 minutes before beginning the rest of the cake. The ganache mixture needs to be chilled prior to baking.

In a bowl, place 1 cup dark chocolate chips or a baking bar broken into pieces. (For dark chocolate chips, I like to use a Ghirardelli bar broken into pieces.)

1. Bring the heavy cream up to a boil, then mix it into the chocolate to melt the chips completely, until smooth.
2. Chill the ganache in the fridge for at least 20 minutes.

While the lava mixture is chilling, begin to prep the cake mixture.

(cont'd)

1. In a bowl, add the dark chocolate chips and butter for the cake mixture.
2. Melt the chocolate and butter in the microwave in 30-second intervals. Mix as you go until the chocolate has completely melted. Set it aside.
3. In a separate bowl, mix the remaining cake mixture ingredients—the eggs, egg yolks, light brown sugar, salt, and vanilla extract. Mix the ingredients with a hand mixer until they are completely integrated.
4. Add the melted chocolate mixture using a wooden spoon or spatula, mixing until the chocolate is fully incorporated.
5. Add the all-purpose flour, also mixing it in by hand.

It's time to prepare the ramekins and add the cake mixture.

1. Preheat the oven to 425°F.
2. Smear a layer of softened butter inside 8 ramekins. Make sure to coat the ramekins with the butter completely. This will help make releasing the cakes from the ramekins easier and leave a lovely glaze on the cakes.
3. Coat the inside of the buttered ramekins by rolling sugar around.
4. Pour the cake mixture into a ramekin halfway.
5. Add a spoon of the chilled lava ganache, then add more cake mixture to cover the ganache completely. Repeat for each ramekin.
6. Bake the cakes for 12 minutes.
7. Using a hand sifter, add powdered sugar on top. Garnish with your favorite berries and ice cream on top or on the side. You can also sprinkle some rock salt for a sweet-and-salty twist.

CHOCOLATE-PEANUT CLUSTERS

By Michael Farmer

YIELD: 4 DOZEN | PREP TIME: 10 MINUTES + COOLING | COOK TIME: 5 MINUTES + COOLING

INGREDIENTS

2 pounds white candy coating, coarsely chopped
1 12-ounce package semisweet chocolate chips
1 11 ½-ounce package milk chocolate chips
5 cups salted dry-roasted peanuts

INSTRUCTIONS

1. In a heavy saucepan over low heat, cook and stir the candy coating and chocolate chips until melted and smooth. Cool the chocolate for 10 minutes.
2. Stir in the peanuts.
3. Once mixed, drop the peanut clusters by rounded tablespoons onto waxed paper–lined baking sheets.
4. Refrigerate the clusters until firm, about 45 minutes.

ELLIOT'S FAVORITE GINGERBREAD COOKIES

By Michelle Coulombe

SERVES: 24 COOKIES | PREP TIME: 20 MINUTES | DOUGH REST TIME: 2–8 HOURS | COOK TIME: 7–10 MINUTES

INGREDIENTS

The Cookies

3 cups all-purpose flour
1 ½ teaspoons baking powder
¾ teaspoon baking soda
¼ teaspoon salt
1 teaspoon ground ginger
3 teaspoons ground cinnamon
¼ teaspoon ground cloves
6 tablespoons unsalted butter
¾ cup brown sugar
1 large egg
½ cup molasses
2 teaspoons vanilla

The Icing

3 cups confectioners' sugar
½ teaspoon vanilla extract
2 teaspoons light corn syrup
4–5 tablespoons water
Pinch of salt

(cont'd)

INSTRUCTIONS

I modified a gingerbread cookie recipe I found online to be more pleasing to the palate of a preschooler. We cut back on the ginger and added cinnamon. These cookies are soft and delicious! They also keep really well—for at least a week in an airtight container. My son Elliot says these are his favorite cookies. And decorating them together is a favorite Christmas tradition.

1. In a small bowl, whisk together the flour, baking powder, baking soda, salt, ginger, cinnamon, and cloves until the ingredients are well blended.
2. In a large bowl, beat the butter, brown sugar, and egg with a hand mixer on medium speed until slightly pale and light.
3. Add the molasses and vanilla, and continue to mix until they are evenly incorporated.
4. Gradually stir the dry ingredients into the wet ingredients until the dough is blended and smooth. Don't overstir.
5. Divide the dough in half, and wrap each half in plastic wrap. Let the dough stand at room temperature for at least 2 hours or up to 8 hours. (The dough can be stored in the refrigerator for up to 4 days. Return it to room temperature before using it.)
6. Preheat the oven to 375°F. Prepare baking sheets by lining them with parchment paper or greasing them lightly.
7. Place 1 portion of the dough on a lightly floured surface. Sprinkle flour over both the dough and a rolling pin. Roll the dough to a scant ¼" thick. Use additional flour to avoid sticking. Cut out cookies with a desired cutter—the teddy bear, gingerbread man, snowflake, and Christmas tree are our favorite shapes.
8. Space the cookies 1 ½" apart on the prepared baking sheets. Bake 1 sheet at a time for 7–10 minutes. (The shorter time will give you softer cookies, which we like!)
9. Remove the cookie sheet from the oven, and allow the cookies to stand until they are firm enough to move to a wire rack.

10. As the cookies cool, whiskthe icing ingredients together. To check for proper consistency, lift the whisk and let the icing drizzle back into the bowl. The ribbon of icing will hold its shape for a few seconds before melting back into the icing if the icing is the correct consistency. Add more confectioners' sugar or water as needed.
11. Put the icing in a ziplock bag, and cut one corner to decorate. We like white icing, but feel free to tint the icing with food coloring. It can be messy, but it's fun to decorate these! Enjoy!

FLAN (INSTANT POT)

By Maritza Escalante

SERVES: 6 | PREP TIME: 10 MINUTES | COOK TIME: 17 MINUTES

INGREDIENTS

The Caramel

½ cup granulated sugar

The Flan Mixture

1 12-ounce can evaporated milk

1 14-ounce can sweetened condensed milk

1 13.5 can coconut cream (optional)

4 eggs

2 tablespoons of your favorite rum or 1 tablespoon vanilla extract

For the Instant Pot

3 cups water

INSTRUCTIONS

The Caramel

1. *Caramelize the sugar:* Heat the sugar in a skillet over medium-high heat. Stir the sugar constantly. It will first start to clump, but once it begins getting hot enough, it will start to turn a golden brown and melt into a caramel. Continually stir until all the sugar has been liquefied and there are no more clumps left in the skillet. Do not leave the stove. The caramel can go from perfect to burnt in the blink of an eye!
2. *Pour the caramel into the flan mold:* Once all the clumps are gone, immediately pour the caramel into the flan mold. Leaving the caramel on the stove any longer could cause it to burn. When pouring the caramel into the flan mold, make sure that it is spread evenly across the bottom of the entire mold.

(cont'd)

3. *Coat the flan mold:* Very carefully rotate the mold so that the caramel will also cover the sides of the mold as well. The caramel is extremely hot and can cause severe burns if you get it on yourself, so make sure to always handle it very carefully. Keep rotating the caramel until it cools and hardens to the point that it no longer moves around.
4. *Set the mold aside:* Set the flan mold aside, and allow the caramel to cool.

The Flan Mixture

1. *Blend the ingredients:* Add the evaporated milk, condensed milk, coconut cream, eggs, and rum (or vanilla extract) to a blender. Blend the ingredients on high speed until fully mixed.
2. *Add to flan mold:* Pour the flan mixture into the flan mold, over the caramel coating. Place and fasten the cover over the flan mold. If you don't have a covered flan mold like I do, use foil to cover the flan. (See the equipment notes below.)

Cooking and Cooling the Flan

1. *Set the 16-minute cook time:* Pour 3 cups of water into the Instant Pot. Use a trivet (or stainless steel official wire roasting rack, compatible with 6-quart cookers), and set the covered flan mold in the Instant Pot. Cook the flan on *Manual High Pressure* for 16 minutes. (The *Manual* button is labeled *Pressure Cook* on some models.)
2. *Cooling the flan:* Once the 16-minute cooking time has completed, allow for a full "natural pressure release" (NPR). After the NPR has finished and the pressure pin has dropped, open the Instant Pot and carefully remove the flan mold. Set it on the counter to cool for 10 minutes before placing in the refrigerator. Refrigerate the flan for at least 3 hours. I know it's hard to wait, but please don't skip this step. Letting the flan sit in the refrigerator overnight will give the best results!

Unmold and Serve

1. *Unmold the flan:* After the flan has been refrigerated for at least 3 hours (or overnight), run a knife along the sides of the mold, separating the flan from the edges of the mold. Use a plate to carefully flip the flan over and expose the beautiful caramel covered dessert.
2. Serve and enjoy!

Equipment Notes

I use the following flan mold, available on Amazon: “EasyShopForEveryone Stainless Steel Flan Mold 63 oz, Ergonomic Handle for Easy Lifting, Compatible with Instant Pot 6 qt, Pot in Pot Cooking, Pressure Cooker, Baking Accessories.”

MILKY WAY CAKE

By Blair Gavitt

SERVES: 12 | PREP TIME: 30 MINUTES | COOK TIME: 70 MINUTES

INGREDIENTS

1 cup pecans, chopped
2 sticks margarine (not butter)
2 cups sugar
4 eggs
2 ½ cups flour (plus more for dusting the pan)
⅛ teaspoon salt
½ teaspoon baking soda
1 cup buttermilk
5 Milky Way bars (Yes, 5!)
1 teaspoon vanilla

INSTRUCTIONS

1. Grease a 10" angel food pan or Bundt pan. Flour it well.
2. Toast the pecans at 325°F for 10–15 minutes.
3. In a large bowl, blend the margarine and sugar together.
4. Add the eggs one at a time, beating well after each addition.
5. In a separate bowl, sift the flour and salt together.
6. In another bowl (or large measuring cup), combine the baking soda with the buttermilk.
7. In several batches (to avoid overworking the batter and to ensure the cake will rise), add the flour and buttermilk alternately to margarine mixture, stirring gently. Start and end with the flour.

8. Melt the Mars Bars in the microwave. I do it in 30-second increments at half power. (I tried using a double boiler, but for some reason, the microwave works better.)
9. Mix the candy into the cake mixture.
10. Add the vanilla and toasted pecans.
11. Bake the cake for 70 minutes.

OLIVE OIL CAKE

By Andrew Daniel

SERVES: 10–12 SLICES | PREP TIME: 10 MINUTES | COOK TIME: 30–35 MIN.

INGREDIENTS

1 ¾ cups flour
1 ½ teaspoons baking powder
7 tablespoons butter, melted
3 tablespoons milk
¾ cup extra-virgin olive oil
4 eggs
1 cup sugar
Zest of 2 lemons or oranges (optional)
Powdered sugar and a rosemary sprig (for garnish)

INSTRUCTIONS

1. Preheat the oven to 350°F.
2. Butter and flour a 10" round cake pan, and line it with parchment paper
3. Sift together the flour and baking powder in a small bowl, and set it aside.
4. Whisk together the melted butter, milk, and olive oil in small bowl, and set it aside.
5. Combine the eggs, sugar, and zest in a medium bowl, and beat them together with an electric mixer until the mixture is light and creamy, about 3–5 minutes.
6. Add some of the flour mixture to the egg mixture, and beat together until incorporated. Then add some of the olive oil mixture into the egg mixture, and beat until incorporated. Keep alternating the flour and olive oil mixtures into the eggs a little at a time until they are all added.
7. Pour the batter into the prepared pan.
8. Bake the cake for 30–35 minutes (depending on strength of your oven)
9. Let the cake completely cool, then dust it with powdered sugar and garnish it with a sprig of rosemary.

PEANUT BUTTER COOKIES

By Cheryl Hatlevig

SERVES: 36| PREP TIME: 30 MINUTES | COOK TIME: 45–50 MINUTES

INGREDIENTS

2 ½ cups (12 ½ ounces) unbleached all-purpose flour
½ teaspoon baking soda
½ teaspoon baking powder
½ teaspoon salt
1 cup (2 sticks) salted butter, softened (it must be softened; it makes a difference in the end product)
1 cup (7 ounces) packed dark brown sugar (or ½ cup light brown sugar and ½ cup dark brown sugar will work; cookies may appear lighter in color after baking if you use only light brown sugar)
1 cup (7 ounces) granulated sugar
1 cup extra-crunchy peanut butter, at room temperature
2 large eggs
2 teaspoons vanilla extract
1 cup (8 ounces) roasted peanuts, ground in a food processor (about 14 pulses) to resemble bread crumbs
1 bag Reece's peanut butter chips (like chocolate chips, only peanut butter)
12 ounces melting milk chocolate almond bark

INSTRUCTIONS

1. Adjust the oven racks to the upper-middle and lower-middle positions, and preheat the oven to 350°F. Line 2 large baking sheets with parchment paper. (Parchment on your baking sheets makes cleanup a breeze.)
2. Whisk the flour, baking soda, baking powder, and salt together in a medium bowl. Set the mixture aside.
3. In a stand mixer fitted with the paddle attachment, beat the butter and sugars at medium speed until light and fluffy, about 2 minutes, scraping

the bowl and beater as needed with a rubber spatula. Add the peanut butter, and mix until it is fully incorporated, about 30 seconds. Add the eggs, one at a time, and the vanilla, and mix until combined, about 30 seconds. Decrease the speed to low, and add the dry ingredients, mixing until combined, about 30 seconds. Mix in the ground peanuts until just incorporated. Remove the bowl from the stand mixer, and scrap the sides and bottom to incorporate all the peanuts. Add the Reece's peanut butter chips, and mix them in by hand until they are incorporated. (This step counts as an arm workout with a personal trainer!)

4. Divide the dough into 36 portions, each a generous 2 tablespoons (a generous ⅛ cup or a medium dough scoop). Roll each portion between your hands to form a ball, about 2" in diameter. Place the dough balls on the prepared baking sheets, spacing them about 2 ½" apart. To make a crisscross design, press each dough ball twice, at perpendicular angles, with a dinner fork dipped in cold water. (To keep the fork cold, I rotate between two forks: one in use, one in the freezer.)
5. Bake the two sheets of cookies—switching the sheets between oven racks and rotating the sheets 180°, for even cooking, halfway through the baking time—until the cookies are puffy and slightly brown around the edges but not on the top, about 10–12 minutes. The cookies will not look fully baked, but, trust me, they are ready. Cool the cookies on the baking sheets for 5 minutes; then, using a wide, metal spatula, transfer the cookies to a wire rack or cool countertop covered with parchment.
6. Microwave the melting chocolate, according to the package instructions, in a bowl deep enough to immerse ½ of a cookie. Dip a cooled cookie into the chocolate, drain the excess chocolate, and lay the cookie back on a parchment-covered cool baking sheet. Refrigerate the dipped cookies for quick chocolate hardening.
7. The cookies can be packed in a container and frozen for storage—or for hiding from family members and guests who like sweets!

In the words of my ninety-three-year-old mother, who IS an expert baker who taught me everything I know about baking, "These are wonderful!" I accept that praise at the level of winning an Emmy or Grammy.

REESE'S PEANUT BUTTER CHEESECAKE

By Shawnae McKown

SERVES: 16 | PREP TIME: 40 MINUTES | COOK TIME: 70 MINUTES

INGREDIENTS

The Oreo Crust

2 cups Oreo crumbs (approximately 24 Oreo cookies)

¼ cup unsalted butter, melted

The Cheesecake Filling

32 ounces cream cheese, softened

1 ⅓ cups sugar

1 cup smooth peanut butter

⅓ cup heavy cream

2 teaspoons vanilla

4 large eggs

1 ¼ cups mini chocolate chips

The Milk Chocolate Ganache

½ cup heavy cream

1 ½ cups milk chocolate chips

Garnish

Reese's cups, coarsely chopped

Peanuts, chopped (optional)

(cont'd)

INSTRUCTIONS

1. First, coat a 9" springform pan with cooking spray, and line the bottom with parchment paper.
2. Wrap the pan with 2 layers of aluminum foil, and bring the foil up the sides of the pan. Make sure it is tight and secure so that no water gets in during the baking in the water bath.

The Oreo Crust

1. *In a food processor, finely grind the whole Oreo cookies, including the cream fillings, to get fine crumbs (about 2 cups).*
2. Combine the crumbs with the melted butter, and stir until they are evenly moistened.
3. Press the mixture into the bottom of the springform pan, and set the crust in the fridge to firm while making the filling.

The Cheesecake Filling

1. Preheat the oven to 350°F.
2. Beat the softened cream cheese with the sugar until smooth.
3. Mix in the peanut butter, heavy cream, and vanilla.
4. Add the eggs one at a time, beating after each addition, just to combine. Stir in the chocolate chips.
5. Spread the mixture over the chilled crust, and smooth the top.
6. Place the springform pan in a roasting pan. Pour hot water into a roasting pan, about a quarter of the way up the springform pan.
7. Bake the cheesecake for 55–70 minutes, until it is set around the edges and slightly loose in the center. Tent the top of the springform pan with aluminum foil if the cheesecake starts browning too quickly.
8. Remove the cheesecake from the water bath, and set it on a cooling rack. Once it is cool, remove the aluminum foil, and refrigerate the cheesecake at least 5 hours or overnight.
9. When the cheesecake has completely cooled, run a thin knife around the edge, and release the ring of the springform pan. Then transfer the cheesecake to a serving plate.

The Milk Chocolate Ganache

1. Over medium heat, bring the heavy cream to a boil. Place half of the milk chocolate chips in a heatproof boil, and pour the cream over the chocolate, stirring until the chocolate has completely melted. Add the remaining chocolate, and stir until it has melted and is smooth. Set the ganache aside to cool; before being added to the cheesecake, the ganache should be pourable but not too thin.
2. Spread the ganache on top of the cheesecake and over the edges. Let it drip down the sides. I suggest doing this in 2 layers to avoid the ganache running down too much. If the ganache won't drip enough, you can slightly reheat the second batch and drizzle it with a spoon. Let the ganache sit slightly, then pile the coarsely chopped Reese's on top. You can also add chopped peanuts if you want. (I didn't!)
3. Set the cheesecake in the fridge until ready to serve.

STRAWBERRY SHORTCAKE

By Daniel Aguilar

SERVES: 6 | PREP TIME: 70 MINUTES | COOK TIME: 18–20 MINUTES

INGREDIENTS

1 ½ pounds strawberries, stemmed and quartered
5 tablespoons sugar (divided)
2 cups all-purpose flour
2 teaspoons baking powder
¼ teaspoon baking soda
¾ teaspoon salt
1 ½ cups heavy cream
Whipped cream

INSTRUCTIONS

1. Mix the strawberries with 3 tablespoons of the sugar. Refrigerate the strawberries, while the juices develop, for at least 30 minutes (or preferably 2 hours).
2. Preheat the oven to 400°F.
3. In a medium bowl, sift together the flour, baking powder, baking soda, remaining 2 tablespoons sugar, and salt. Add the heavy cream, and mix until just combined. Place the mixture in an ungreased 8" square pan, and bake it until golden, 18–20 minutes.
4. Remove the shortcake from the pan, and place it on a rack to cool slightly. Cut it into 6 pieces, and split each piece in half horizontally.
5. Spoon some of the strawberries with their juice onto each shortcake bottom. Top with a generous dollop of whipped cream and then the shortcake top. Spoon more strawberries over the top, and serve.

SUMMER BERRY TRIFLE

By Deanna Brownley

SERVES: 12 | PREP TIME: 15 MINUTES | ASSEMBLY TIME: 5 MINUTES

INGREDIENTS

Berries

6 heaping cups strawberries, stemmed
1 tablespoon sugar
Blueberries (optional)

1 prepared angel food cake

The Cream Cheese Layer

2 8-ounce packages cream cheese, softened
1 cup heavy whipping cream
2 teaspoons vanilla
2 tablespoons powdered sugar

Whipped Cream

1 cup heavy whipping cream
3 tablespoons powdered sugar
1 teaspoon vanilla

(W)

INSTRUCTIONS

1. Slice the strawberries in half, into triangles, and place them into a large bowl. Sprinkle them with the sugar, and toss to combine. (I added blueberries to the trifle pictured below, as this was a Fourth of July dessert.)
2. Slice the angel food cake into three even layers/circles.
3. *To make the cream cheese layer:* In a mixing bowl, combine the softened cream cheese, cream, vanilla, and powdered sugar. Mix until a spreadable, frosting-like consistency is formed. Add more cream if needed. *To make the whipped cream:* In a large mixing bowl, combine the cream, powdered sugar, and vanilla. Whip until soft peaks form—do not overmix.
4. *To assemble the trifle:* In a large, shallow bowl (or trifle bowl), begin with a layer of the angel food cake. Fill the hole of the cake with a few strawberries, then insert some strawberries along sides (as pictured). Then spread ⅓ of the cream cheese mixture, then ⅓ of the mixed fruit.
5. Repeat for the next two layers, finishing with a layer of whipped cream.
6. Chill and serve.

ZUCCHINI BREAD

By Pauline Lacroix

YIELD: 2 LOAVES | PREP TIME: 15 MINUTES | COOK TIME: 60 MINUTES

INGREDIENTS

3 large eggs
1 cup vegetable oil
2 cups granulated sugar
2 cups packed grated zucchini
1 tablespoon vanilla
1 teaspoon baking soda
1 teaspoon salt
¼ teaspoon baking powder
½ teaspoon allspice
1 tablespoon cinnamon
3 cups flour
½ cup walnuts, chopped
1 cup raisins

INSTRUCTIONS

1. Preheat the oven to 325°F.
2. In a large bowl, beat the eggs till light.
3. Beat in the oil and sugar.
4. Add in the zucchini and vanilla, and mix.
5. Mix in all the dry ingredients, then add in the nuts and raisins.
6. Pour the batter into two greased loaf pans, and bake for 60 minutes or until an inserted toothpick comes out dry.